MARK W. BASS

Saving Souls

Presented as a compilation, *n.*   the action or process of
producing something, especially a list, book, or report,
by assembling information collected from other sources.

SAVING SOULS

First published: 2012

Second edition: 2019

Printed by The Baesman Group in Hilliard, Ohio of U.S.A.

ISBN: 978-0-615-43110-9

Library of Congress Control Number: 2011900379

Quotes from _The Way of Divine Love_, copyright 1949 Sands & Co. Ltd., 3 Trebeck St. London, W.1, England; Dissolved in 1991; Public domain work.

Quotes from _DIARY, Saint Maria Faustina Kowalska, Divine Mercy in My Soul,_ copyright 1987 Congregation of Marians of the Immaculate Conception, Stockbridge, MA 01263; Used with permission.

Devine_Mercy_Vilnius-2011 Image Jesus, I Trust in You; Used with permission of the Marian Fathers of the Immaculate Conception of the B.V.M.

Order information
Go to markwbass.com

I dedicate this book to Jeanne and Joseph Barnes.

In 1978 God let me fall in love with and marry their oldest daughter, Mary Barnes.

In 1985 Mary's mother and father gave me a Bible.

In 1986 her father Joe asked if I had opened it yet?

In 1987 he asked if I knew where it was?

In 1988 he asked if I had tried to read it?

In 1989 he asked how I could not read the most read book in the world?

In 1990 he asked if I had lost it?

In 1991 he suggested I start with the New Testament.

In 1992 I opened the Bible to the first Gospel of Matthew and started reading.

Isn't it wonderful how God works.

There are six billion copies of the *Bible* in print (and counting).

Billy Graham wrote a 14 page (3 inch by 4 ½ inch) pamphlet titled *Steps to Peace With God* because he feels the Divine Knowledge in the *Bible* is so important that he would prioritize and simplify it just in case you have not bought one yet or you have one and reading all 1,424 pages proves to be too difficult. Mr. Graham does a wonderful job with his words and use of scripture of how we can have peace with God now on earth and eternally in heaven.

There are millions (they are not keeping count) of copies of *Steps to Peace With God* in print (and counting). Go to billygraham.org or call toll free 877-247-2426 and order one if you have not read it.

Rick Warren wrote a 319 page book titled *The Purpose Driven Life* because he feels the same way as Billy Graham. Mr. Warren does a wonderful job with his words and use of scripture of bringing the *Bible* into the 21st century in a very practical way.

There are fifty two million copies of *The Purpose Driven Life* in print (and counting). Go to any bookstore and buy one if you have not read it.

My goal is the same as theirs but of two Divine Writings of the 20th century.

The cover of *The Way of Divine Love*, copyright page, introduction, picture and biography of Sister Josefa Menendez are shared on pages 2, 3, 4, & 5
and
the cover of *Divine Mercy in My Soul*, copyright page, preface, picture and biography of Saint Maria Faustina Kowalska are shared on pages 6, 7, 8, & 9.

THE WAY OF
DIVINE LOVE

By Sister Josefa Menéndez

NIHIL OBSTAT:

Patricius Morris, S.T.D., L.S.S.
Censor Deputatus

IMPRIMATUR:

E. Morrogh Bernard, Vic. Gen.
Westmonasterii, die 5a Maii, 1953

Reprinted by arrangement with the copyright holder:

Sands & Co. (Publishers), Ltd.
3 Trebeck Street
London, W.I. England

Library of Congress Catalog Card No. 79-112493

ISBN: 0-89555-030-X

The first edition, 1949, went through seven printings in England. The revised edition, April, 1955, has been printed ten times. First American printing by TAN Books and Publishers, Inc., was February, 1972. Subsequent printings by TAN Books and Publishers, Inc., were in October, 1975; May, 1977; August, 1978; April, 1979 and January, 1981.

PRINTED AND BOUND IN THE UNITED STATES OF AMERICA

TAN BOOKS AND PUBLISHERS, INC.
P.O. Box 424
Rockford, Illinois 61105

1981

Sister Josefa's book contains 482 pages and there are 480,000 copies in print (and counting).

Below is part of the introduction written on pages xvi and xvii in her book.

Jesus, the Word Incarnate, has transmitted in all its completeness the Message He Himself received from the Father: *"Omnia quaecumque audivi a Patre Meo, nota feci vobis"* (John XV, 15). There is nothing to add to Our Lord's words, and at the death of St. John, the last Apostle, the divine revelation was closed and sealed. Later ages could do no more than draw out its meaning. But its riches are unfathomable, and most men are too inattentive and superficial to sound the depths of the Gospel teaching; consequently, just as under the *Old Law* Prophets were sent by God to revive the faith and hope of His people, so in the *New Dispensation* Christ has from time to time given certain chosen souls the mission of interpreting His authentic words, and of revealing their depths and hidden meaning.

Long ago, on Easter morning, He charged Saint Mary Magdalen with announcing His glorious Resurrection to the Apostles. In succeeding ages likewise poor and humble women have been chosen out to transmit His most important desires to mankind.

To recall only the chief instances: Through Saint Juliana of Montcornillon He revived devotion to the Blessed Sacrament, and obtained the institution of the Feast of Corpus Christi; through Saint Margaret Mary a new stimulus was given to devotion to the Sacred Heart; through Saint Thérèse of the Child He told a world which seemed to have forgotten it the merit and value of spiritual Childhood, and now, He has given a Message to Josefa Menéndez.

"His ways are not our ways, nor His thoughts our thoughts," and that there may be no doubt that the communications come from Him and no other, He chooses weak instruments, humanly speaking unfitted for the task in view; so His strength shines forth in their infirmity.

He did not choose the learned and the great in the world's eyes to found His Church, Saint Paul expressly tells us, otherwise the rapid spread of Christianity could have been attributed to their talents and prestige... but He chose the poor and the ignorant, and of these He made vessels of election.

(Signed) H. Monier Vinard S.J.

June 11, 1921
Society of the Sacred Heart
Convent of Les Feuillants, Poitiers.   France

Jesus appears to Sister Josefa Menéndez

p. 98   "I want you to write and to keep all I say to you. It will be read when
you are in heaven."

Above text is on page 98 in her book.

Sister Josefa Menéndez
Born 1890 in Madrid, Spain.
Josefa was the oldest of four girls, her father Leonardo and mother Lucia.
Every Sunday the whole family went to High Mass followed by country walks.
Celebrating First Communion at the age of eleven, she heard a voice
"Yes, little one I want you to be all Mine."
As a child Josefa attended the Sacred Heart Free School, which was not far from
her home. Later Josefa received training in a millinery establishment for dressmaking.
As a clever dressmaker and with more orders than she could fill, she organized a workroom
and there trained a number of young girls. After her father died in 1910 Josefa wanted more and
more to be a nun but her mother asked that she stay near the family.
In 1919 and 29 years of age a Noviceship for sisters opened in one of the French houses of the
Sacred Heart at the Convent of Les Feuillants, Poitiers.
Without hesitation, Josefa accepted.
Died 1923 in Poitiers, France.

Divine Mercy in My Soul

of Saint Maria Faustina Kowalska

Sister Faustina's book contains 1,828 diary entries and there are 4,600,000 copies in print (and counting).

Below is part of the preface written on page xii in her book.

The reader, after just a superficial skimming of the *Diary*, may be struck by the simplicity of the language and even by the spelling and stylistic errors, but he should not forget that the author of the *Diary* had but a limited elementary education. The theology alone which is found in the *Diary* awakens in the reader a conviction of its uniqueness; and if one considers the contrast between [Saint] Faustina's education and the loftiness of her theology, the contrast alone indicates the special influence of Divine Grace.

I would like to mention here my meeting with a well-known contemporary mystic, Sister Speranza, who in Collevalenza, not far from Todi [Italy], founded the sanctuary of "The Most Merciful Love," the site of numerous pilgrimages. I asked Sister Speranza whether she had heard of the writings of Sister Faustina and what she thought of them. She answered me with simplicity: "The writings contain a wonderful teaching, but reading them one must remember that God speaks to philosophers in the language of philosophers and to simple souls in the language of the simple ones, and only to these last does He reveal truths hidden from the wise and prudent of this world."

+Andrew M. Deskur
Titular Archbishop of Tene

June 4, 1937
Congregation of Sisters of Our Lady of Mercy
Warsaw, Poland

Sister Maria Faustina Kowalska heard a voice

> **1142** **My daughter, be diligent in writing down every sentence I tell you concerning My mercy, because this is meant for a great number of souls who will profit from it.**

Above text is entry 1142 in her diary.

Saint Maria Faustina Kowalska
Born 1905 in Glogowiec, Poland.
Helen (name given at birth) was the third of ten children, her father Stanislaus
and mother Marianne. When she was only seven, Helen hears for the first time
a voice in her soul, calling her to a more perfect way of life.
At the age of twelve she begins her primary education. Less than three years later
Helen leaves her family to work as a domestic for the Bryszewski family
in the nearby city of Aleksandrow. This was to help her family who was poor and to
earn her own livelihood. Helen begins to share with her parents her interest to be a nun.
Needing more help, her parents ask that she continue to work. Helen travels to another nearby
city Lodz and for the next couple of years works for three terciaries and
then later a store. In 1925 and 20 years of age Helen heard these words from Jesus
Go at once to Warsaw; you will enter a convent there.
She applies to the Congregation of Sisters of Our Lady of Mercy and is accepted.
A year later Helen will bear her name in religion, Sister Maria Faustina.
Died 1938 in Cracow, Poland.

For you to know my words and those of Jesus, Sister Josefa, and Sister Faustina,
I will continue to cut and paste all text from these two Divine Writings.
Each of Sister Josefa's writings are preceded by the page number from her book and each
of Sister Faustina's writings are preceded by the diary entry number from her book.
I want as little credit as possible.
Also in Sister Faustina's diary, words spoken by Jesus are in bold print and words spoken
by the Mother of God (Mary) are in italic print.

The Holy Spirit and the Catholic Church put the *Bible* together during the first 4 centuries, AD.
The *Bible* is a collection of 52 books and 21 letters inspired by God and written by men.
The Holy Spirit and Mark Bass (me) put this book, *Saving Souls* together in the 21st century.
Saving Souls is a collection of 2 books dictated by Jesus and written by 2 women.

The Holy Spirit and I took our favorite text from the 1,117 pages of these 2 books written
in the 20th century, and have brought them into the 21st century in 67 pages.

Given the text is written by two Catholic nuns, in Catholic Convents, it does have a Catholic feel,
but the Divine Knowledge is from Jesus, thus it is a Christian message to all souls.

Both "private revelations" have been approved by the Catholic Church.
The Congregation for the Doctrine of the Faith in Rome reviewed and gave permission to
publish both works. On April 30th, 2000 Pope John Paul II canonized Sister Maria Faustina
Kowalska as Saint Maria Faustina Kowalska.
There is a same current effort for Sister Josefa Menéndez.

Jesus is alive and well and still in the business of saving souls.
These new Divine Writings tell us how we can help.
This is what this book is.

The Holy Spirit and I put this book together because odds are you have not read either *The Way of Divine Love* or *Divine Mercy in My Soul*. With 5,080,000 copies in print combined and 7.6 billion people in the world, only 1 in 1,496 has a copy of either one, less of both.

When Jesus tells Sister Josefa "It will be read when you are in heaven." we do not want to let Jesus or Sister Josefa down, we need to read it.

When Jesus tells Sister Faustina **this is meant for a great number of souls** I am sure Jesus' definition of a great number is more than ½ the people in the world.

7.6 billion x .5 + 1 =   3,800,000,001 (a great number)

So, to reach this great number the Holy Spirit, I, and Oprah Winfrey (will someone please call her) need to print and distribute 38,000,001 copies.

Then 38,000,001 people need to pray for 100 family, friends, neighbors, co-workers, and others. I started with my 80 year old father who was an atheist and in poor health.

Jesus allowed his soul to let go of his worn out body at 12 noon on Jesus' birthday of 2009. How's that for the power of prayer. I suggest praying for the older, possible non-believers first. I am currently at 376 family, friends, neighbors, co-workers, and others. (and counting)

OK, are you ready to team up with Jesus Christ, Sister Josefa Menéndez, and Saint Maria Faustina Kowalska to get souls to heaven?

Get out of our way Satan, with God/Jesus/Holy Spirit (Trinity) there is no stopping us now!

AMEN!!

PS: The Holy Spirit said in my heart, "Double it", meaning print and distribute 76,000,002.

First order of business.
As described in the *Bible*, **heaven** and **hell** do exist.

From Jesus to Sister Faustina

777 (**187**) November 27, [1936]. Today I was in heaven, in spirit, and I saw its inconceivable beauties and the happiness that awaits us after death. I saw how all creatures give ceaseless praise and glory to God. I saw how great is happiness in God, which spreads to all creatures, making them happy; and then all the glory and praise which springs from this happiness returns to its source; and they enter into the depths of God, contemplating the inner life of God, the Father, the Son, and the Holy Spirit, whom they will never comprehend or fathom.

This source of happiness is unchanging in its essence, but it is always new, gushing forth happiness for all creatures. Now I understand Saint Paul, who said, "Eye has not seen, nor has ear heard, nor has it entered into the heart of man what God has prepared for those who love Him."

741   Today, I was led by an Angel to the chasms of hell. It is a place of great torture; how awesomely large and extensive it is! The kinds of tortures I saw; the first torture that constitutes hell is the loss of God; the second is perpetual remorse of conscience; the third is that one's condition will never change; (**160**) the fourth is the fire that will penetrate the soul without destroying it – a terrible suffering, since it is a purely spiritual fire, lit by God's anger; the fifth torture is continual darkness and a terrible suffocating smell, and, despite the darkness, the devils and the souls of the damned see each other and all the evil, both of others and their own; the sixth torture is the constant company of Satan; the seventh torture is horrible despair, hatred of God, vile words, curses and blasphemies. These are the tortures suffered by all the damned together, but that is not the end of the sufferings. There are special tortures destined for particular souls. These are the torments of the senses. Each soul undergoes terrible and indescribable sufferings, related to the manner in which it has sinned. There are caverns and pits of torture where one form of agony differs from another. I would have died at the very sight of these tortures if the omnipotence of God had not supported me. Let the sinner know that he will be tortured throughout all eternity, in those senses which he made use of to sin. (**161**) I am writing this at the command of God, so that no soul may find an excuse by saying there is no hell, or that nobody has ever been there, and so no one can say what it is like.

I, Sister Faustina, by the order of God, have visited the abysses of hell so that I might tell souls about it and testify to its existence. I cannot speak about it now; but I have received a command from God to leave it in writing. The devils were full of hatred for me, but they had to obey me at the command of God. What I have written is but a pale shadow of the things I saw. But I noticed one thing: that most of the souls there are those who disbelieved that there is a hell. When I came to, I could hardly recover from the fright. How terribly souls suffer there! Consequently, I pray even more fervently for the conversion of sinners. I incessantly plead God's mercy upon them. O my Jesus, I would rather be in agony until the end of the world, amidst the greatest sufferings, than offend You by the least sin.

p. 141   It was in the night of Wednesday to Thursday, 16th March, that Josefa made her mysterious descent into hell for the first time.

From the 6th of March, soon after Our Lord's disappearance, infernal voices had several times caused her great fear and disturbance of mind.

p. 142   Damned souls, invisible to her eyes, came from... the lowest depths, reproaching her for her want of generosity. She was greatly perturbed... She heard cries of despair like these; "I am there where love is banished... for ever... how brief was the enjoyment... and the punishment is eternal... What have I gained?... hate, and that for ever... eternal hatred!"

p. 143   "In the night of 16th March towards ten o'clock," wrote Josefa, "I became aware, as on the preceding days, of a confused noise of cries and chains. I rose quickly and dressed, and trembling with fright, knelt down near my bed. The uproar was approaching, and not knowing what to do, I left the dormitory, and went to our Holy Mother's cell; then I came back to the dormitory. The same terrifying sounds were all round me; then all of a sudden I saw in front of me the devil himself.

" 'Tie her feet and bind her hands,' he cried...

"Instantly I lost sight of where I was, and felt myself tightly bound and being dragged away. Other voices screamed: 'No good to bind her feet; it is her heart that you must bind.'

" 'It does not belong to me,' came the answer from the devil.

"Then I was dragged along a very dark and lengthy passage, and on all sides resounded terrible cries. On opposite sides of the walls of this narrow corridor were niches out of which poured smoke, though with very little flame, and which emitted an intolerable stench. From these recesses came blaspheming voices, uttering impure words. Some cursed their bodies, others their parents. Others, again reproached themselves with having refused grace, and not avoided what they knew to be sinful. It was a medley of confused screams of rage and despair. I was dragged through that kind of corridor, which seemed endless. Then I received a

p. 144   violent punch which doubled me in two, and forced me into one of the niches. I felt as if I were being pressed between two burning planks and pierced through and through with scorching needle points. Opposite and beside me souls were blaspheming and cursing me. What caused me most suffering... and with which no torture can be compared, was the anguish of my soul to find myself separated from God...

"It seemed to me that I spent long years in that hell, yet it lasted only six or seven hours... Suddenly I was violently pulled out of the niche, and I found myself in a dark place; after striking me, the devil disappeared and left me free... How can I describe my feelings on realizing that I was still alive, and could still love God!

"I do not know what I am not ready to endure to avoid hell, in spite of my fear of pain. I see clearly that all the sufferings of earth are nothing in comparison with the horror of no longer being able to love, for in that place all breathes hatred and thirst to damn other souls."

She hesitated to tell all she saw and heard in that abode of sorrow, for her soul was dismayed by its horrors. However, she tried to speak and Our Lady appeared to her on Wednesday, 25th October, and told her that by so doing she was carrying out God's plan:

"My child, I come to tell you in the name of Jesus how much glory you gave His Heart to-day… You must understand that all He allows you to see and suffer in hell is meant not only to purify you, but also that you should pass on the knowledge of it to the Mothers. Do not think about yourself but only of the glory given to the Heart of Jesus, and the salvation of souls."

Night after night she spent almost wholly in these torments, and Josefa wrote in great sorrow on November 5th:

"I saw souls fall into hell in dense groups, and at times it was impossible to calculate their number."

This left her terror-stricken and exhausted.

"Unless I am given special help from on high, I shall no longer be able either to work or apply myself to anything…"

On Sunday after one of these terrible nights of expiation Our Lord came to her. She was in dire desolation of spirit, and spoke to Him of the innumerable souls lost for ever. Jesus listened and His face betrayed immense sadness. After a few moments of silence, He said: "You have seen the fallen, Josefa, but you have not yet seen those who are saved and go up into heaven!"

"Then," she wrote, "I saw an innumerable crowd of souls, rank upon rank, and they entered into an illimitable space which was filled with resplendent light, and were lost in immensity."

The Heart of Jesus was as if on fire and He said: "All those are they who have accepted the Cross of My love, and accomplished My will with submission."

After a few moments, He came back to the subjects of expiation and reparation which He wanted Josefa to undertake, and He explained their value to her:

"As to the time during which I allow you to undergo the pains of hell, do not for a moment consider it as lost and useless. Sin is an offence against God's infinite Majesty, which therefore calls for infinite reparation. When you go down into the abyss, your sufferings prevent the loss of many souls, the Divine Majesty accepts them in satisfaction for the outrages received from these souls and they repair for the punishment their sins have merited. Never lose sight of the fact that it is only My great love for you and for souls that permits it."

Josefa would not forget it, and it seemed as if she were coming back to the hardest trials of her Noviceship days in the storms that now assailed her. Foreseeing that now the love of Christ's Heart was to be poured out over the whole world, the devil's fury made him fiercely attack the instrument used by Our Lord, but he was not able to shake her lowliness or her trust.

"I hate you," he said to her, "with all the hatred of hell, and I will pursue you until I have driven you from that accursed house…" "How many souls she snatches from me"–he one day acknowledged–"and if she is able to do this now, what will it be later on?… No, I will put an end to this undertaking, I will get hold of her confounded writings and burn them… I will use my power… but she is as strong as death!"

Josefa remained unshakable. "I got back my peace of soul with the Mothers," she wrote simply.

Oh, and to those of you who think the Catholic Church made up **purgatory** wrong.

From Jesus to Sister Faustina

20   Shortly after this, I fell ill [general exhaustion]. The dear Mother Superior sent me with two other sisters for a rest to Skolimow, not far from Warsaw. It was at that time that I asked the Lord for whom else should I pray for. Jesus said that on the following night He would let me know for whom I should pray.

[The next night] I saw my Guardian Angel, who ordered me to follow him. In a moment I was in a misty place full of fire in which there was a great crowd of suffering souls. They were praying fervently, but to no avail, for themselves; only we can come to their aid. The flames which were burning them did not touch me at all. My Guardian Angel did not leave me for an instant. I asked these souls what their greatest suffering was. They answered me in one voice that their greatest torment was longing for God. I saw Our Lady visiting the souls in Purgatory. The souls call her "The Star of the Sea." She brings them refreshment. I wanted to talk with them some more, but my Guardian Angel beckoned me to leave. We went out of that prison of suffering. [I heard an interior voice] which said, **My mercy does not want this, but justice demands it.** Since that time, I am in closer communion with the suffering souls.

p.148   There were other mysteries beyond the pale that were revealed to Josefa during this period of Lent 1922.

Whilst day and night she bore the burden of these terrible persecutions, God put her in touch with another abyss of woe, that of purgatory. Many souls came to solicit her suffrages and sacrifices in terms of very great humility. At first she was frightened, but by degrees she became accustomed to their confidences. She listened to them, asked them their names, encouraged them, and very humbly recommended herself to their intercession. The lessons they inculcated are worth remembering.

One of them came to announce her deliverance and said: "The important thing is not entrance into religion, but entrance into the next world." "If religious souls but realized the heavy price to be paid for concessions to the body…" said another, while asking for prayers. "My exile is at an end and I am going to my eternal home…"

A priest-soul said to her: "How great is the mercy of God, when He deigns to make use of the sufferings of other souls to repair our infidelities; what a degree of glory I might have acquired had my life been different."

It was a nun who, on her entrance into heaven, confided to Josefa: "How different the things of earth appear when one passes into eternity. What are charges and offices in the sight of God? All He counts is the purity of our intention when exercising them, even in the smallest acts. How little is the earth and all it contains, and yet, how loved… Ah! What comparison is there between life, however prolonged, and eternity. If only it were realized how in purgatory the soul is wearied and consumed with desire to see God."

There were also some poor souls, who having escaped through God's mercy from a still greater peril, came to beg Josefa to hasten their deliverance.

p.149   "I am here by God's great mercy," one of them said, "for my excessive pride had brought me to the gates of hell. I influenced a great number of other people, and now I would gladly throw myself at the feet of the most abject pauper.

"Have compassion on me and do acts of humility to make reparation for my pride, thus you will be able to deliver me from this abyss."

"I spent seven years in mortal sin," another confessed, "and three years ill in bed, and I always refused to go to confession. I was ripe for hell-fire and would have fallen into it if by your present sufferings you had not obtained for me the grace of repentance. I am now in purgatory, and I entreat you, since you were able to save me… draw me out of this dreary prison."

"I am in purgatory because of my infidelity, for I would not correspond with God's call," said another. "For twelve years I held out against my vocation and was in the greatest peril of damnation, because in order to stifle my conscience I gave myself up to a life of sin. Thanks to the divine goodness, which deigned to make use of your sufferings, I took courage to come back to God… and now, of your charity, get me out of this gloomy prison."

"Offer the Blood of Christ for us," said another who was just about to leave purgatory. "What would become of us, if there were no one to help us?"

The names of these holy souls, who were personally unknown to Josefa, having been carefully noted down with the date and place of their decease, were more than once verified. The assurance thereby gained of the truth of the facts she related remains as a precious testimony of her intercourse with purgatory.

p. 83   During meditation on Spy Wednesday, 23rd March, she asked Him in her prayer what exactly He meant by "saving souls".

"He came," she said, "and looked at me with great affection. He replied: "There are some Christian souls and even very pious ones that are held back from perfection by some attachment. But when another offers Me her actions united to My infinite merits, she obtains grace for them to free themselves and make a fresh start.

" 'Many others live in indifference and even in sin, but when helped in the same way, recover grace, and will eventually be saved.

" 'Others again, and these very numerous, are obstinate in wrongdoing and blinded by error. They would be damned if some faithful soul did not make supplication for them, thus obtaining grace to touch their hearts, but their weakness is so great that they run the risk of a relapse into their sinful life; these I take away into the next world without any delay, and that is how I save them.'

"I asked Him how I could save a great many.

" 'Unite all you do to My actions, whether you work or whether you rest. Unite your breathing to the beating of My Heart. How many souls **you**[1] would be able to save that way.'"

So be the faithful soul, and say a prayer of supplication for your family, friends, neighbors, co-workers, and others.

Random House Dictionary
supplication,   n.   the act of supplicating; humble prayer, entreaty, or petition.

Important Note: Jesus says   **you**[1]
as a Team.
as God did with Noah, Moses, Abraham, Kings David & Solomon, and Esther.
as Jesus did with Matthew, Mark, Luke, John, Paul, Timothy, James, and Peter.
You see God/Jesus/Holy Spirit love working with and through us.
The Trinity is the One winning wars, healing people, driving away Satan, and saving souls.

p. 38   This Heart again showed Itself to her on 16th September. She heard: 'To satisfy a love so great, you must try to find souls for Me. You will do so by suffering and by love. You will have to bear many humiliations, but do not be afraid, for you are in My Heart.' "

p. 68   What you need is to forget self, to abandon your own will and offer no resistance to My plans. Thanks to the acts done in the midst of your sufferings, several of the souls that you will see later have come nearer to My Heart.' "

p. 69   Love, suffer, and obey. So doing you will enable Me to carry out My plans in you.' "

p. 71   The First Friday of February was the anniversary of her arrival at Poitiers. Jesus appeared to her, and showing her His Heart all aglow,

p. 72   He said: "Every Friday, and especially on the first of the month, I will make you share in the bitterness of My Heart, and you shall endure the torments of My Passion in a special way." 1

" 'In these days when hell opens to engulf so many I want you to offer yourself as a victim, so as to save the greatest possible number of souls.'

"He stayed a few minutes more, but in silence, and then vanished."

p. 118   "On Thursday, 1st September," wrote Josefa, "He came after communion. When He began to speak His voice was very sad.

" 'I want you to comfort Me.,' He said. 'Great is the coldness of souls… and how many blindly throw themselves into hell. I should like to leave you My Cross as I used to do.'

"Afterwards, when I had asked leave, He led me to the oratory of Saint Stanislaus and there He said: 'If I were unable to find souls to solace Me and draw down mercy, justice could no longer be restrained.'

"A little later, He continued: 'My love for souls is so great that I am consumed with desire to save them. But O! how many are lost, and how numerous are those who are waiting for the sacrifices and sufferings that are to obtain for them the grace to forsake their evil ways… However, I still have many souls who love Me and belong to Me. A single one of them can purchase pardon for a great many others who are cold and ungrateful.

" 'I want **you**[1] to burn with desire to save souls. I want you to throw yourself into My Heart and to make My glory your sole occupation.

474　　In the evening, when I was in my cell, I saw an Angel, the executor of divine wrath. He was clothed in a dazzling robe, his face gloriously bright, a cloud beneath his feet. From the cloud, bolts of thunder and flashes of lightning were springing into his hands; and from his hand they were going forth, and only then were they striking the earth. When I saw this sign of divine wrath which was about to strike the earth, and in particular a certain place, which for good reasons I cannot name, I began to implore the Angel to hold off for a few moments, and the world would do penance. But my plea was a mere nothing in the face of the divine anger. Just then I saw the Most Holy Trinity. The greatness of Its majesty pierced me deeply, and I did not dare to repeat my entreaties. At that very moment I felt in my soul the power of Jesus' grace, which dwells in my soul. When I became conscious of this grace, I was instantly snatched up before the Throne of God. Oh, how great is our Lord and God and how incomprehensible His holiness! I will make no attempt to describe this greatness, because before long we shall all see Him as He is. I found myself pleading with (**197**) God for the world with words heard interiorly.

　　As I was praying in this manner, I saw the Angel's helplessness: he could not carry out the just punishment which was rightly due for sins. Never before had I prayed with such inner power as I did then.

475　　The words with which I entreated God are these: **Eternal Father, I offer You the Body and Blood, Soul and Divinity of Your dearly beloved Son, Our Lord Jesus Christ for our sins and those of the whole world; for the sake of His sorrowful Passion, have mercy on us.**

476　　The next morning, when I entered chapel, I heard these words interiorly: **Every time you enter the chapel, immediately recite the prayer which I taught you yesterday.** When I had said the prayer, in my soul I heard these words: **This prayer will serve to appease My wrath. You will recite it for nine days, on the beads of the rosary, in the following manner: First of all, you will say one OUR FATHER and HAIL MARY and the I BELIEVE IN GOD. Then on the OUR FATHER beads you will say the following words: "Eternal Father, I offer You the Body and Blood, Soul and Divinity of Your dearly beloved Son, Our Lord Jesus Christ, in atonement for our sins and those of the whole world." On the HAIL MARY beads you will say the following words: "For the sake of His sorrowful Passion have mercy on us and on the whole world." In conclusion, three times you will recite the words: "Holy God, Holy Mighty One, Holy Immortal One, have mercy on us and on the whole world."**[100]

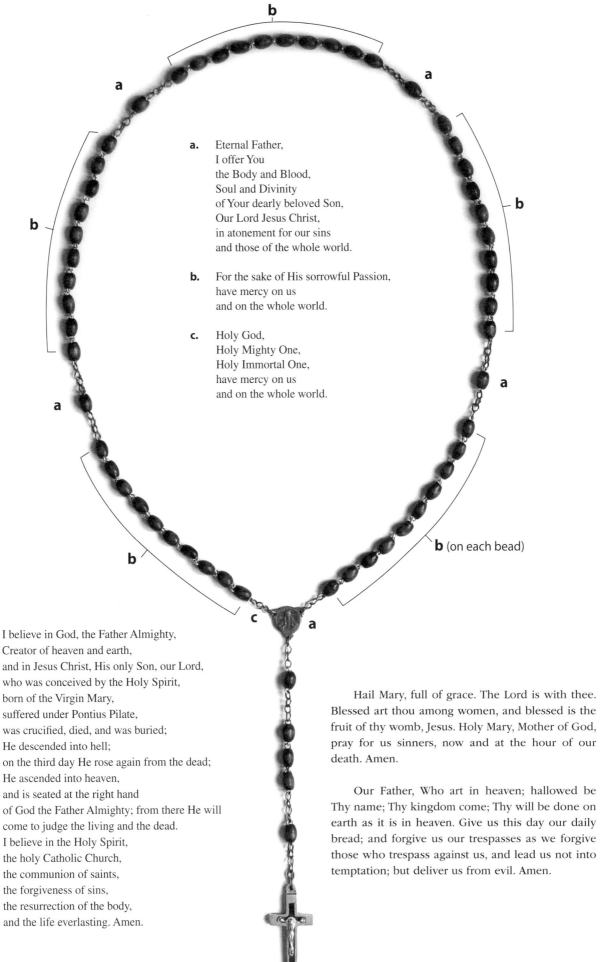

a. Eternal Father,
I offer You
the Body and Blood,
Soul and Divinity
of Your dearly beloved Son,
Our Lord Jesus Christ,
in atonement for our sins
and those of the whole world.

b. For the sake of His sorrowful Passion,
have mercy on us
and on the whole world.

c. Holy God,
Holy Mighty One,
Holy Immortal One,
have mercy on us
and on the whole world.

b (on each bead)

I believe in God, the Father Almighty,
Creator of heaven and earth,
and in Jesus Christ, His only Son, our Lord,
who was conceived by the Holy Spirit,
born of the Virgin Mary,
suffered under Pontius Pilate,
was crucified, died, and was buried;
He descended into hell;
on the third day He rose again from the dead;
He ascended into heaven,
and is seated at the right hand
of God the Father Almighty; from there He will
come to judge the living and the dead.
I believe in the Holy Spirit,
the holy Catholic Church,
the communion of saints,
the forgiveness of sins,
the resurrection of the body,
and the life everlasting. Amen.

Hail Mary, full of grace. The Lord is with thee. Blessed art thou among women, and blessed is the fruit of thy womb, Jesus. Holy Mary, Mother of God, pray for us sinners, now and at the hour of our death. Amen.

Our Father, Who art in heaven; hallowed be Thy name; Thy kingdom come; Thy will be done on earth as it is in heaven. Give us this day our daily bread; and forgive us our trespasses as we forgive those who trespass against us, and lead us not into temptation; but deliver us from evil. Amen.

687   Once, as I was going down the hall to the kitchen, I heard these words in my soul: **Say unceasingly the chaplet that I have taught you. Whoever will recite it will receive great mercy at the hour of death. Priests will recommend it to sinners as their last hope of salvation. Even if there were a sinner most hardened, if he were to recite this chaplet only once, he would receive grace from My infinite mercy. I desire that the whole world know My infinite mercy. I desire to grant unimaginable graces to those souls who trust in My mercy.**

811   When I entered my solitude, I heard these words: **At the hour of their death, I defend as My own glory every soul that will say this chaplet; or when others say it for a dying person, the indulgence is the same. When (205) this chaplet is said by the bedside of a dying person, God's anger is placated, unfathomable mercy envelops the soul, and the very depths of My tender mercy are moved for the sake of the sorrowful Passion of My Son.**

1128   May 22, 1937. The heat is so intense that it is difficult to bear. We are all thirsting for rain, and still it does not come. For several days the sky has been overcast, but there is no rain. When I looked at (**35**) the plants, thirsting for the rain I was moved with pity, and I decided to say the chaplet until the Lord would send us rain. Before supper, the sky covered over with clouds, and a heavy rain fell on the earth. I had been saying this prayer without interruption for three hours. And the Lord let me know that everything can be obtained by means of this prayer.

1541   **My daughter, encourage souls to say the chaplet which I have given to you. It pleases Me to grant everything they ask of Me by saying the chaplet. When hardened sinner say it, I will fill their souls with peace, and the hour of their death will be a happy one.**

    Write this for the benefit of distressed souls; when a soul sees and realizes the gravity of it sins, when the whole abyss of the misery into which it immersed itself is displayed before its eyes, let it not despair, but with trust let it throw itself into the arms of My mercy, as a child into the arms of its beloved mother. These souls (125) have a right of priority to My compassionate Heart, they have first access to My mercy. Tell them that no soul that has called upon My mercy has been disappointed or brought to shame. I delight particularly in a soul which has placed its trust in My goodness.

    Write that when they say this chaplet in the presence of the dying, I will stand between My Father and the dying person, not as the just Judge but as the merciful Savior.

I am thinking you do not have to be Catholic to say the chaplet but if you are Apostolic, Baptist, Episcopal, Lutheran, Methodist, Presbyterian, or a Non-Denominational Evangelical you will probably be more comfortable being that faithful soul referred to by Jesus to Sister Josefa.

I am also thinking both prayers were given to two nuns at different times and places in history and each by itself accomplishes the same goal, eternity with God in heaven with your family, friends, neighbors, co-workers, and others.

You are thinking my Lord and my God, so as faithful souls all of our humble prayers we have been saying over the past two thousand years really have helped countless souls get into Your kingdom of heaven.

You are also thinking   nice.

(**18**) + February 22, 1931

47   In the evening, when I was in my cell, I saw the Lord Jesus clothed in a white garment. One hand [was] raised in the gesture of blessing, the other was touching the garment at the breast. From beneath the garment, slightly drawn aside at the breast, there were emanating two large rays, one red, the other pale. In silence I kept my gaze fixed on the Lord; my soul was struck with awe, but also with great joy. After a while, Jesus said to me, **Paint an image according to the pattern you see, with the signature: Jesus, I trust in You. I desire that this image be venerated, first in your chapel, and [then] throughout the world.**

48   **I promise that the soul that will venerate this image will not perish. I also promise victory over [its] enemies already here on earth, especially at the hour of death. I Myself will defend it as My own glory.**

313   +Once, when I was visiting the artist [Eugene Kazimirowski] who was painting the image, and saw that it was not as beautiful as Jesus is, I felt very sad about it, but I hid this deep in my heart. When we had left the artist's house, Mother Superior [Irene] stayed in town to attend to some matters while I returned home alone. I went immediately to the chapel and wept a good deal. I said to the Lord, "Who will paint You as beautiful as You are?" Then I heard these words; **Not in the beauty of the color, nor of the brush lies the greatness of this image, but in My grace.**

Random House Dictionary

venerate,   v.   to regard or treat with reverence; revere.

Jesus, I Trust in You

299   When, on one occasion, my confessor told me to ask the Lord Jesus the meaning of the two rays in the image,[77] I answered, "Very well, I will ask the Lord."

During prayer I heard these words within me: **The two rays denote Blood and Water. The pale ray stands for the Water which makes souls righteous. The red ray stands for the Blood which is the life of souls...**

These two rays issued forth from the very depths of My tender mercy when My agonized Heart was opened by a lance on the Cross.

These rays shield souls from the wrath of My Father. Happy is the one who will dwell in their shelter, for the just hand of God shall not lay hold of him. I desire that the first Sunday after Easter be the Feast of Mercy.

326   Once, Jesus said to me, **My gaze from this image is like My gaze from the cross.**

1789   (**136**) + Today[253] I saw the glory of God which flows from the image. Many souls are receiving graces, although they do not speak of it openly. Even though it has met up with all sorts of vicissitudes, God is receiving glory because of it; and the efforts of Satan and of evil men are shattered and come to naught. In spite of Satan's anger, The Divine Mercy will triumph over the whole world and will be worshiped by all souls.

Please take the liberty to remove this image page from your book, frame, mount it on a dry board, or tape it as it is high on a wall, and venerate it per Jesus' desire.
Or
Go to www.marian.org or call Marian Helpers in Stockbridge, MA, at 800-462-7426 and order this Vilnius Divine Mercy Image on paper board stock or canvas, framed or unframed, and available in many sizes.

49   When I told this to my confessor,[29] I received this for a reply: "That refers to your soul." He told me, "Certainly, paint God's image in your soul." When I came out of the confessional, I again heard words such as these: **My image already is in your soul. I desire that there be a Feast of Mercy. I want this image, which you will paint with a brush, to be solemnly blessed on the first Sunday after Easter; that Sunday is to be the Feast of Mercy.**

699   On one occasion, I heard these words: **My daughter, tell the whole world about My inconceivable (138) mercy. I desire that the Feast of Mercy[139] be a refuge and shelter for all souls, and especially for poor sinners. On that day the very depths of My tender mercy are open. I pour out a whole ocean of graces upon those souls who approach the Fount of My Mercy. The soul that will go to Confession and receive Holy Communion shall obtain complete forgiveness of sins and punishment. On that day all the divine floodgates through which graces flow are opened. Let no soul fear to draw near to Me, even though its sins be as scarlet. My mercy is so great that no mind, be it of man or of angel, will be able to fathom it throughout all eternity. Everything that exists has come forth from the very depths of My most tender mercy. Every soul in its relation to Me will contemplate My love and mercy throughout eternity. The Feast of Mercy emerged from My very depths of tenderness. (139) It is My desire that it be solemnly celebrated on the first Sunday after Easter. Mankind will not have peace until it turns to the Fount of My Mercy.**

742   **My daughter, if I demand through you that people revere My mercy, you should be the first to distinguish yourself by this confidence in My mercy. I demand from you deeds of mercy, which are to arise out of love for Me. You are to show mercy to your neighbors always and everywhere. You must not shrink from this or try to excuse or absolve yourself from it.**

       I am giving you three ways of exercising mercy toward your neighbor: the first–by deed, the second–by word, the third–by prayer. In these three degrees is contained the fullness of mercy, and it is an unquestionable proof of love for Me. By this means a soul glorifies and pays reverence to My mercy. Yes, the first Sunday after Easter is the Feast of Mercy, but there must also be acts of mercy, and I demand the worship of My mercy through the solemn celebration of the Feast and through the veneration of the image which is painted. By means of this image I shall grant many graces to souls. It is to be a reminder of the demands of My mercy, because even the strongest (163) faith is of no avail without works. O my Jesus, You Yourself must help me in everything, because You see how very little I am, and so I depend solely on Your goodness, O God.

1320   At three o'clock, implore My mercy, especially for sinners; and, if only for a brief moment, immerse yourself in My Passion, particularly in My abandonment at the moment of agony. This is the hour of great mercy for the whole world. I will allow you to enter into My mortal sorrow. In this hour, I will refuse nothing to the soul that makes a request of Me in virtue of My Passion...

1572   I remind you, My daughter, that as often as you hear the clock strike the third hour, immerse yourself completely in My mercy, adoring and glorifying it; invoke its omnipotence for the whole world, and particularly for poor sinners; for at that moment mercy was opened wide for every (145) soul. In this hour you can obtain everything for yourself and for others for the asking: it was the hour of grace for the whole world – mercy triumphed over justice.

p. 88

"...I went up to the oratory of Our Lady in the Noviceship to implore her not to let me fall. She came, at once, very motherly and said:

"My daughter, I will give you a lesson of very great importance: 'the devil is like a mad dog, but he is chained, that is to say, his liberty is curtained. He can, therefore, only seize and devour his prey if you venture too near him, and that is why his usual tactics are to make himself appear as a lamb. The soul does not realize this, and draws nearer and nearer, only to discover his malice when in his clutches. When he seems far away, do not relax your vigilance, child; his footsteps are padded and silent, that he may take you unawares.'

p. 89

"She gave me her blessing and went away."

p. 125

A new trial was added in the night of 4th December. Pulled violently from her bed, she was thrown to the ground, under the fiendish blows. Long hours were so spent, and the torture renewed on the two following nights. After one such terrible night, she wrote on the morning of Tuesday, 6th December:

"Unable to bear any more, I knelt beside my bed. Suddenly I heard gnashing of teeth and a yell of rage. Then all vanished and before me stood Our Lady, all loveliness.

" 'Do not fear, my daughter; I am here.'

"I told her how terrified I was of the devil, who made me suffer so much.

" 'He may torment you, but he has no power to harm you. His fury is very great on account of the souls that escape him... souls are of such great worth... If you but knew the value of a soul...'

"Giving me her blessing, she said: 'Do not fear.' I kissed her hand and she went away."

p. 185

The Feast of the Assumption did not end without a visit from the Mother of God, and she, too, reminded Josefa that Jesus meant to make use of her very misery to further His great work.

It was while Josefa and her sisters were saying the rosary in the oratory of the Noviceship that she appeared:

"She was clothed," said Josefa, "as on the day of my vows, a diadem crowned her head, her hands were crossed on her breast and a little wreath of white roses encircled her heart.

p. 186

" 'These flowers will be changed into pearls of great price for the salvation of souls,' she said, looking first at the novices kneeling round her statue."

And then turning to Josefa: "Yes, souls are what Jesus loves most; I, too, love them for they are the price of His Blood and so many are lost for ever. Do not resist His will, daughter, and never refuse Him anything He asks of you. Surrender yourself wholly to the work of His Heart which is none other than the salvation of souls."

p. 256   "You thus acquire a relationship with My Mother, who being a mortal creature was nevertheless of spotless purity… subject to all human miseries, yet at every instant of her life absolutely immaculate. She has glorified Me more than all the celestial spirits, and God Himself, drawn by her purity, took flesh of her and dwelt in His creature.

p. 269   She had hardly reached her cell when she was joined by Our Lady. "What pleases My Son most is love and humility–so write:

p. 270   "Josefa," He said to her that night, "is it true that you would like something to say to My Mother that would please her? Write what I tell you."

"Then in ardent, burning, even enthusiastic words," she noted, He said this prayer:

" 'O tender and loving Mother, most prudent Virgin, Mother of my Redeemer, I come to salute you to-day with all the love that a child can feel for its mother.

" 'Yes, I am indeed your child, and because I am so helpless I will take the fervour of the Heart of your Divine Son; with Him I will salute you as the purest of creatures, for you were framed according to the wishes and desires of the thrice-holy God.

" 'Conceived without sin, exempt from all corruption, you were ever faithful to the impulses of grace, and so your soul accumulated such merit that it was raised above all other creatures.

" 'Chosen to be the Mother of Jesus Christ, you kept Him as in a most pure sanctuary, and He who came to give life to souls, Himself took life from you, and received nourishment from you.

" 'O incomparable Virgin! Immaculate Virgin! Delight of the Blessed Trinity, admiration of all angels and saints, you are the joy of heaven. Morning Star, Rose blossoming in springtime, Immaculate Lily, tall and graceful Iris, sweet-smelling Violet. Garden enclosed kept for the delight of the King of heaven… you are my Mother, Virgin most prudent, Ark most precious containing every virtue! you are my Mother, most powerful Virgin, Virgin clement and faithful you are my Mother, O Refuge of sinners! I salute you and rejoice at the sight of the gifts bestowed on you by the Almighty, and of the prerogatives with which He has crowned you!

p. 271

" 'Be blessed and praised, Mother of my Redeemer, Mother of poor sinners! Have pity on us and cover us with your motherly protection.

" 'I salute you in the name of all men, of all saints and all angels.

"Would that I could love you with the love and fire of the seraphim, and this is too little to satisfy my desires… and to render you filial homage constant and pure for all eternity.

" 'O incomparable Virgin, bless me, since I am your child. Bless all men! Protect them and pray for them to Him who is almighty and can refuse you nothing.

" 'Adieu, tender and sweet Mother; day and night I salute you, in time and for eternity.'

"Now, Josefa, praise the Mother with the words of the Son, and the Son with those of His Mother."

"Never," said Josefa, "had I seen His Heart so resplendent, nor heard in His voice such burning enthusiasm!"

p. 383 The feast of the Assumption of Our Blessed Lady, 15th August 1923, brought another short interval of radiant happiness to Josefa, for towards evening on that glorious day Our Lady appeared in all her beauty. With motherly love, she listened to Josefa's troubles, to her fears for the future on account of her frailty and weakness.

"Daughter," she replied, "do not be discouraged by your weakness, acknowledge it in all humility, but always with confidence, because you know well that Jesus made choice of you for the very reason of your misery and worthlessness... so be humble, but also very trustful."

And alluding to the devil's increasing persecutions: "Do not be afraid, for he can only do one thing, that is, give you opportunities of increasing your merit. Do you not know that I am watching over you and that Jesus will never abandon you?"

So Josefa threw off the burden of her personal preoccupations to rejoice in the bliss of her heavenly Mother, of whom the whole world was celebrating the Assumption into heaven.

A thrill of joy transfused the face of Our Lady, as she recalled the beatitude of the eternal present she now possessed.

p. 384 " 'Today,' she said, 'in very truth, there began for me a beatitude which was perfect and unalloyed, for during the whole of my life in this world my soul was transpierced by a sword of grief.'

" 'I asked her,' " wrote Josefa naively, " 'if the presence of the Child Jesus, so small and so lovely, had not been the best of consolations?'

" 'Listen, child,' " Our Lady went on. " 'From childhood I knew of divine things and the hopes centered in the coming of the Messiah. So when the Angel declared the mystery of the Incarnation to me, and I found myself chosen as the Mother of the Redeemer of mankind, though my heart adhered to the divine will with entire submission, it was drowned in a sea of bitterness and woe. For I knew all that this tender and heavenly Child was destined to endure, and Simeon's prophecy only confirmed the anguish of my mother's heart.

" 'Can you, then, imagine how I felt while contemplating My Son's charms, His heavenly countenance, His hands and feet which I knew were to be so cruelly ill-treated?

" 'I kissed those little hands, and felt my lips already stained with the Precious Blood that one day would gush from their wounds.

" 'I kissed His feet, and already saw them nailed to the Cross.

" 'And as I carefully tended His hair, I pictured it all clotted with Blood and entangled in the cruel thorns.

" 'And when at Nazareth, He first ventured on a few steps, hastening with outstretched arms to meet me, my tears fell as I pictured them extended on the Cross on which He was to die.

" 'When He reached boyhood, He was so divinely beautiful that none could contemplate Him unmoved... yet in my heart, the heart of a mother, the sword was turned at the thought of the tortures that were to be inflicted on Him, of which I felt beforehand the savage recoil.

" 'Then He left me for three years during His apostolic life, and there followed the terrible hours of His Passion and Death. What a martyrdom!

" 'When after three days I saw Him in the glory of His risen life the trial changed, for I knew that He could suffer no more... but O! how sad it was to part from Him! My sole relief then lay in consoling Him, by repairing for the sins of men. And my long

p. 385 exile began… How I sighed for the hour of everlasting union… What was life without Him?… How dim was my light!… How ardent my desires!… How long, long, He was in coming!

" 'I was about to enter my seventy-third year, when my soul passed like a flash from earth to heaven. At the end of three days the Angels fetched my body and brought it in triumph and jubilation to reunite it to my soul… What adoration!… What admiration!… What sweetness, when at long last my eyes beheld in glory His Majesty surrounded by the angelic choirs… my Son… my God!

" 'And how, daughter, can I express the amazement of my lowliness when I was crowned with such gifts and overwhelmed with jublilations and rejoicings?… Sorrow had indeed passed away, never to return… For all eternity, glory, sweetness and love were mine.' "

625   In the evening, when I was praying, the Mother of God told me, *Your lives must be like Mine: quiet and hidden, in unceasing union with God, pleading for humanity and preparing the world for the second coming of God.*

635   March 25. In the morning, during meditation, God's presence enveloped me in a special way, as I saw the immeasurable greatness of God and, at the same time, His condescension to His creatures. Then I saw the Mother of God, who said to me, *Oh, how pleasing to God is the soul that follows faithfully the inspirations of His grace! I gave the Savior to the world; as for you, you have to speak to the world about His great mercy and prepare the world for the Second* (91) *Coming of Him who will come, not as a merciful Savior, but as a just Judge. Oh, how terrible is that day! Determined is the day of justice, the day of divine wrath. The angels tremble before it. Speak to souls about this great mercy while it is still the time for* [granting] *mercy. If you keep silent now, you will be answering for a great number of souls on that terrible day. Fear nothing. Be faithful to the end. I sympathize with you.*

1414   The Feast of the Immaculate Conception. Before Holy Communion I saw the Blessed Mother inconceivably beautiful. Smiling at me She said to me, *My daughter, at God's command I am to be, in a special and exclusive way your Mother; but I desire that you, too, in a special way, be My child.*

1415   *I desire, My dearly beloved daughter, that you practice the three virtues that are dearest to Me–and most pleasing to God. The first is humility; humility, and once again humility; the second virtue, purity; the third virtue, love of God. As My daughter, you must especially radiate with these virtues.* When the conversation ended, She pressed me to Her Heart and disappeared. When I regained the use of my senses, (45) my heart became so wonderfully attracted to these virtues; and I practice them faithfully. They are as though engraved in my heart.

1711   When I was left alone with the Blessed Virgin, She instructed me concerning the interior life. She said, *The soul's true greatness is in loving God and in humbling oneself in His presence, completely forgetting oneself and believing oneself to be nothing, because the Lord is great, but He is well-pleased only with the humble, He always opposed the proud.*

From Jesus to Sister Josefa

p. 142   This time Our Lord sent Saint Madeleine Sophie as His messenger.

On Tuesday, 14th March, she appeared to Josefa in her cell. After listening to her humble avowals, she gave her fresh courage, and heartened her with the words: "Remember, daughter, that nothing happens unless it is in God's designs."

p. 150   In the afternoon on Holy Thursday, 13th April, 1922, she wrote:

"I was in the Chapel at about half-past three when I saw before me a personage clothed like Our Lord, rather taller, very beautiful and with a wonderful expression of peace on his face which was most attractive. His vesture was of a dark reddish purple. He held in his hand the Crown of Thorns just like the one Our Lord used to bring me long ago.

" 'I am the Disciple of the Lord,' he said, 'John the Evangelist, and I bring you one of the Master's most precious jewels.'

"He gave me the Crown and himself placed it on my head."

Josefa was at first rather startled at this unexpected apparition, but she gained assurance through the feeling of intense peace which took possession of her. She ventured to confide in the saintly visitor, telling him of the anguish the ill-treatment of the devil caused her.

" 'Have no fear,' was the reply. "Your soul is a lily which is kept by Jesus in His Heart–I am sent to make you acquainted with some of the feelings that overwhelmed His Heart on this great day:

" 'Love was about to part Him from His disciples, after it had baptized Him in a baptism of blood. But love urged Him to remain with them, and it was love that made Him conceive the idea of the Blessed Sacrament.

" 'What a struggle then arose in His Heart. He thought of how He would rest in pure souls, but also how His Passion would be carried on in hearts sullied by sin.

" 'How His Heart thrilled at the thought of the moment, then approaching, when He would go to the Father, but it was crushed with sorrow at the sight of one of the Twelve, one specially chosen, who was to deliver Him up to death, and at the knowledge that for the first time His Blood was to prove useless to save a soul.

" 'How His Heart wore itself out in love! But the want of correspondence to grace of those so beloved plunged It into dire distress... and what of the indifference and coldness of so many chosen souls?'

"With these words he was gone."

p. 212 Next day Wednesday, 29th November, while she was waiting for Our Lord and working, suddenly her cell was filled with a soft effulgent light. It was not the Master who had come but the Apostle beloved of His Heart.

"I recognized him at once," she wrote, "he held the Cross of Jesus in his hands. I renewed my vows and he said:

" 'Soul, loved of Our Divine Master, I am John the Evangelist, and I come to bestow His Cross on you. It does not wound the body, but makes the heart bleed... May the suffering it will cause you relieve the bitterness in which sinners steep the Heart of Our Lord and God... May the blood of your heart be as a delicious vintage that will make known to many the sweetness and attractiveness of virginity... Unite your heart to Jesus in all you do. Keep carefully the precious evidences of His love. Fix your eyes on heaven, for the things of earth are of no account. Suffering is the life of the soul and the soul that has understood its value lives the true life."

Josefa had already noted on Holy Thursday, 1922, how heavenly was the expression of St. John's countenance. He was a friend from the other world whom she was to see again many times, and whose every visit left her with a sense of peace and security. The Cross brought this day weighed chiefly on her soul.

p. 350 Before the end of the Octave of the Sacred Heart, Saint Madeleine Sophie gave Josefa some valuable teaching about the motto she had previously given her at Marmoutier: "Love knows no obstacles."

On Sunday, 10th June, she appeared at Josefa's side during Mass, and blessing her, said:

"Daughter, I have come to-day to tell you how to love, so that true love may find no opposition in you.

"The basis of love is humility; for it is often necessary to submit and sacrifice our likes and dislikes, our comfort and our self-love if we wish to give proof of true love... and this act of submission is none other than one of humility, for it is abnegation, self-denial, generosity and adoration in one. In fact, to prove this love in something that costs us very much we have to think in this way: 'If it were not for Thee, O my God, I would not do it. But as it is for Thee, I cannot say no; I love Thee and I submit to Thy will. It is my God who asks this of me, so I must obey. I do not know why He asks it, but *He* knows.' And so because of love we humble ourselves, and with submission do what we do not understand and do not like, unless with a supernatural love and solely because it is the will of God.

"Daughter, it is by loving that you will change interior resistance and any difficulties that occur into love that is humble, strong and generous. Let them be an act of perpetual adoration of the one Lord and God who is Master of all souls. Never resist, never question, never falter. Do what He asks of you; say what He wants you to say, without fear or vacillation or omission. He is All-holy and Wisdom itself, Master and Lord and Love. Adieu, my child."

706   [September] 29. On the Feast of Saint Michael the Archangel, I saw by my side that great Leader, who spoke these words to me: "The Lord has ordered me to take special care of you. Know that you are hated by evil; but do not fear – 'Who is like God!' " And he disappeared. But I feel his presence and assistance.

820   My Guardian Angel told me to pray for a certain soul, and in the morning I learned that it was a man whose agony had begun that very moment. The Lord Jesus makes it known to me in a special way when someone is in need of my prayer. I especially know when my prayer is needed by a dying soul. This happens more often now than it did in the past.

1203   Saint Joseph urged me to have a constant devotion to him. He himself told me to recite three prayers [the Our Father, Hail Mary, and Glory Be] and the *Memorare*[204] once every day. He looked at me with great kindness and gave me to know how much he is supporting this work [of mercy]. He has promised me this special help and protection. I recite the requested prayers every day and feel his special protection.

1442   + When I arrived at Midnight Mass, from the very beginning I steeped myself in deep recollection, during which time I saw the stable of Bethlehem filled with great radiance. The Blessed Virgin, all lost in the deepest of love, was wrapping Jesus in swaddling clothes, but Saint Joseph was still asleep. Only after the Mother of God put Jesus in the manger, did the light of God awaken Joseph, who was also praying. But after a while, I was left alone with the Infant Jesus who stretched out His little hands to me, and I understood that I was to take Him in my arms. Jesus pressed His head against my heart and gave me to know, by His profound gaze, how good He found it to be next to my heart. At that moment Jesus disappeared and the bell was ringing for Holy Communion.

p. 208   Josefa listened and transcribed the grave and burning words that fell from the divine lips.

"I will begin by speaking to My chosen souls, and to all who are consecrated to Me. They must know Me, so as to be able to teach those I shall confide to their care all the kindness and tenderness of My Heart, and to tell all that if I am an infinitely just God, I am none the less an infinitely merciful Father. Let My chosen souls, My spouses, My religious, and priests, teach all poor souls how much I love them! All this I will teach you by degrees, and thus I shall be glorified in your abjection, in your littleness, in your nothingness. I do not love you for what you are… but for what you are not, that is to say, your wretchedness and nothingness, for thus I have found a place for My greatness and bounty."

From Jesus to Sister Faustina.

580   (**47**) On a certain occasion, the Lord said to me, **I am more deeply wounded by the small imperfections of chosen souls than by the sins of those living in the world.** It made me very sad that chosen souls make Jesus suffer, and Jesus told me, **These little imperfections are not all. I will reveal to you a secret of My Heart: what I suffer from chosen souls. Ingratitude in return for so many graces is My Heart's constant food, on the part of [such] a chosen soul. Their love is lukewarm, and My Heart cannot bear it; these souls force Me to reject them. Others distrust My goodness and have no desire to experience that sweet intimacy in their own hearts, but go in search of Me, off in the distance, and do not find Me. This distrust of My goodness hurts Me very much. If My death has not convinced you of My love, what will? Often a soul wounds Me mortally, and then no one can comfort Me. (48) They use My graces to offend Me. There are souls who despise My graces as well as all the proofs of My love. They do not wish to hear My call, but proceed into the abyss of hell. The loss of these souls plunges Me into deadly sorrow. God though I am, I cannot help such a soul because it scorns Me; having a free will, it can spurn Me or love Me. You, who are the dispenser of My mercy, tell all the world about My goodness, and thus you will comfort My Heart.**

592   I learned in the Heart of Jesus that in heaven itself there is a
       heaven to which not all, but only chosen souls, have access. In-
       comprehensible is the happiness in which the soul will be im-
       mersed. O my God, oh, that I could describe this, even in some
       little degree. (**56**) Souls are penetrated by His divinity and pass
       from brightness to brightness, an unchanging light, but never
       monotonous, always new though never changing. O Holy Trin-
       ity, make yourself known to souls!

926   February 9, [1937]. Shrove Tuesday. During the last two days of
       the carnival, I experienced the overwhelming flood of chastise-
       ments and sins. In one instant the Lord gave me a knowledge
       of the sins committed throughout the whole world during these
       days. I fainted from fright, and even though I know the depth of
       God's mercy, I was surprised that God allows humanity to exist.
       And the Lord gave me to know who it is that upholds the exis-
       tence of mankind: it is the chosen souls. When the number of the
       chosen ones is complete, the world will cease to exist.

1601   The Lord has given me to know how much He desires the perfec-
       tion of chosen souls.

       **Chosen souls are, in My hand, lights which I cast into the
       darkness of the world and with which I illumine it. As stars
       illumine the night, so chosen souls (6) illumine the earth.
       And the more perfect a soul is, the stronger and the more
       far-reaching is the light shed by it. It can be hidden and
       unknown, even to those closest to it, and yet its holiness is
       reflected in souls even to the most distant extremities of the
       world.**

From Jesus to Sister Josefa

p. 271   "It is twenty-two years to-day," wrote Josefa (Saturday, 17th March 1923), "since I heard the voice of Jesus for the first time, when I was preparing for my First Communion. I was reminding Him of this during my thanksgiving when suddenly He appeared... such loveliness! His garment seemed of gold and His Heart one blaze of fire... How can I describe It?"

p. 272   " 'Josefa,' I said to you then, 'I want you to be all Mine.' To-day I can say to you: 'You are all Mine.' Then I was preparing to attract you to My Heart... to-day you are imprisoned in It. Come... enter and rest therein, since it is your dwelling."

Then He opened His Heart to admit Josefa... "It was like heaven," she wrote, "and I thought myself no longer on this earth..."

p. 400   She wrote on Monday, 8th October:

"I told Our Lord during my thanksgiving how my soul trembles at the thought of His judgments, now that I see myself on the brink of death and my life laid bare before Him...

"He came quite suddenly and looked at me long and sweetly, with immense tenderness..."

Josefa loved to dwell on Our Lord's look, which of itself gave her such peace. How many souls, when they read of that divine glance of Jesus, will feel faith in His tenderness revivified, for it penetrates, purifies, calms and strengthens. The eyes of Jesus will surely rest on them too; none who believe can doubt this.

When He had, as it were, read Josefa through and through, He said:

"All that is true, if you merely look at what you have done. But, Josefa, I shall Myself introduce you to the citizens of heaven. I am preparing the robe I destine for you. It is woven of the precious flax of My merits and dyed in the purple of My Blood. My lips will seal your soul with the kiss of peace and love. So do not fear, I will not forsake you till I have led you where your soul will rest in everlasting Light."

Josefa's simple comment was; "Jesus has taken away all my fear of death."

p. 436   "That will be our work in heaven, Josefa; to teach souls how to live
p. 437   united in Me, not as if I were far away, but in them, because by grace I dwell in them.

From Jesus to Sister Faustina

707   (**143**) October 2, 1936. The First Friday of the month. After Holy Communion, I suddenly saw the Lord Jesus, who spoke these words to me: **Now I know that it is not for the graces or gifts that you love me, but because My will is dearer to you than life. That is why I am uniting Myself with you so intimately as with no other creature.**

1292   When I received Holy Communion, I said to Him, "Jesus, I thought about You so many times last night," and Jesus answered me, **And I thought of you before I called you into being.** "Jesus, in what way were You thinking about me?" **In terms of admitting you to My eternal happiness.** After these words, my soul was flooded with the love of God. I could not stop marveling at how much God loves us.

1605   **Write down everything that occurs to you regarding My goodness.** I answered, "What do You mean, Lord, what if I write too much?" And the Lord replied, **My daughter, even if you were to speak at one and the same time in all human and angelic tongues, even then you would not have said very much, but on the contrary, you would have sung in only a small measure the praises (9) of My goodness – of My unfathomable mercy.**

O my Jesus, You Yourself must put words into my mouth, that I may praise You worthily.

My daughter, be at peace; do as I tell you. Your thoughts are united to My thoughts, so write whatever comes to your mind. You are the secretary of My mercy. I have chosen you for that office in this life and the next life. That is how I want it to be in spite of all the opposition they will give you. Know that My choice will not change.

1664   During adoration, Jesus said to me, **My daughter, know that your ardent love and the compassion you have for Me were a consolation to Me in the Garden** [of Olives].

1754   **Consider, My daughter, Who it is to whom your heart is so closely united by the vows. Before I made the world, I loved you with the love your heart is experiencing today and throughout the centuries, (117) My love will never change.**

It is three o'clock in the afternoon on a warm and sunny March day during the season of Lent, 2010. I am sitting at my four top table in the Northeast corner of the Bob Evans Restaurant on Riverside Drive, across from Scioto Country Club Golf Course in Columbus, Ohio, USA. My four top, because this is where I most frequently come between lunch and dinner to put this book together with the Holy Spirit. This section of the restaurant is closed during slow hours, but the management has been so kind to allow me this peaceful corner, four windows to the North, three windows to the East, the sounds of light rock-n-roll, wonderful apple dumpling pie, fresh cups of coffee accompanied with many little plastic containers of chilled Half & Half, and the most gracious help. My server Holly is still on maternity leave and the assistant manager Alex wants to buy the first book.

The rest of this book is titled miscellaneous.

This day I have placed four small tin crosses on my table and hold my rosary with the prayer that Jesus will continue to guide me as His humble instrument.

From Jesus to Sister Josefa

p. 91   "Never does My Heart refuse to forgive a soul that humbles itself," He answered, drawing near, "especially when it asks with confidence.

p. 94   "My Heart takes comfort in forgiving. I have no greater desire, no greater joy, than when I can pardon a soul.

p. 211   Then with ardour too intense to be restrained, He began to speak and she gathered up His burning words:

In an admirable epitome of His whole redemptive life, Jesus showed infinite love as the central theme:

"I am all Love! My Heart is an abyss of love.

"It was love that made man and all existing things that they might be at his service.

"It was love that moved the Father to give His Son for man's salvation which through his own fault he had lost.

"It was love that caused a Virgin who was little more than a child to renounce the charms of life in the Temple and consent to become the Mother of God, thereby accepting all the suffering involved in the Divine Maternity.

"It was love that caused Me to be born in the inclemency of winter, poor and destitute of everything.

"It was love that hid Me thirty years in complete obscurity and humble work.

"It was love that made me choose solitude and silence... to live unknown and voluntarily to submit to the commands of My Mother and adopted Father. For love saw how in the course of ages many souls would follow My example and delight in conforming their lives to Mine.

"It was love that made Me embrace all the miseries of human nature, for the love of My Heart saw far ahead. I knew how many imperilled souls would be helped by the acts and sacrifices of others and so would recover life.

"It was love that made Me suffer the most ignominious contempt and horrible tortures... and shed all My Blood and die on the Cross to save mankind and redeem the whole human race.

"And love saw how, in the future, many souls would unite themselves to My torments and dye their sufferings and actions, even the most ordinary, with My Blood in order to win many souls to Me.

"I will teach you all this very clearly, Josefa, that men may know how far-reaching is the love of My Heart for them.

p. 212   "And now go back to your work, and live in Me as I do in you."

p. 112   "Do not let your falls, however many, trouble you. It is trouble and worry that keep a soul from God.

"I want you to be very little and very humble, and always gay. Yes, I want you to live in joy, while endeavouring all the time to be something of an executioner to self. Often choose what costs you, but without loss of joy and gladness, for by serving Me in peace and happiness you will give the most glory to My Heart."

p. 193   " 'I do not look at the act itself, I look at the intention,' He replied. 'The smallest act, if done out of love, acquires such merit that it gives Me immense consolation... I want only love, I ask for nothing else.' "

p. 213   " 'I so much want souls to understand this! It is not the action in itself that is of value; it is the intention with which it is done. When I swept and laboured in the workshop of Nazareth, I gave as much glory to My Father as when I preached during My Public Life.

" 'There are many souls who in the eyes of the world fill important posts and they give My heart great glory; this is true. But I have many hidden souls who in their humble labours are very useful workers in My vineyard, for they are moved by love, and they know how to cover their deeds with supernatural gold by bathing them in My Blood. My love goes so far that My souls can draw great treasure out of mere nothing. When as soon as they wake they unite themselves to Me and offer their whole day with a burning desire that My Heart may use it for the profit of souls... when with love they perform their duties, hour by hour and moment by moment... how great is the treasure they amass in one day!

" 'I will reveal My love to them more and more... it is inexhaustible, and how easy it is for a loving soul to let itself be guided by love.' "

p. 232   That same evening the devil, exasperated by the intervention of the saint, and still more by her advice, exclaimed: "That blessed one will be the ruin of my power, through her humility alone."
And as if forced to reveal his infernal secret—
"Ah!" he roared, blaspheming, "when I want to keep strong hold of a soul, I have only to incite her to pride... and if I want to bring about her ruin, I have only to let her follow the instincts of her pride.

"Pride is the source of my victories and I will not rest till the world is full of it. I myself was lost through pride, and I will not allow souls to save themselves through humility.

"There is no doubt about it," he cried with a yell of rage, "all those who reach highest sanctity have sunk deepest in humility."

p. 234 Encouraged by such condescension, Josefa plied Jesus with her artless questions.

"How is it," she wrote, "that when prayer is made for a soul month after month there seems to be no result?... How is it that He who so longs for the conversion of sinners, leaves their hearts untouched, so that many prayers and sacrifices are lost?... and I spoke to Him of three sinners and especially of two, for whom we have been praying so long!"

"When a soul prays for a sinner with an intense desire for his conversion," Our Lord answered graciously, "his prayer generally obtains the sinner's conversion, though sometimes only at the last moment, and the offence given to My Heart is repaired. But in any case, prayer is never lost, for on the one hand, it consoles Me for the pain sin has occasioned, and on the other, its efficacy and power are applied, if not to that sinner, then to others better disposed to profit by it.

p. 235 Understand this well, Josefa, when a soul loves Me, she can make up for many who offend Me, and this relieves My Heart."

p. 237 "I asked Him if He remembers our faults after we have been sorry for them and have obtained His forgiveness."

" 'As soon as a soul throws itself at My feet and implores My forgiveness, Josefa, I forget all her sins.'

"I asked Him if people will go on offending Him to the end of the world."

" 'Yes, alas... to the end of the world, but I shall also have some who are a comfort to Me.'

"I wanted to know if He does not make His voice heard by souls that are plunged in sin, in order to induce them to change, for I see for myself that when I am in temptation and resist, suddenly I feel within me something that makes me know the truth and at once I am seized with sorrow."

Jesus answered: "Yes, Josefa, I pursue sinners as justice pursues criminals. But justice seeks them in order to punish, I, in order to forgive."

Then as she offered Him as a consolation the desires of religious, which are more than usually ardent during carnival time, He added before leaving her: "My chosen souls are to My Heart as balm to a wound. I will return later, Josefa, go on consoling Me."

p. 286 "Meditate for a moment on the martyrdom of My supremely tender and loving Heart at finding Barabbas preferred to Me, and how, at seeing Myself so scorned, I felt cut to the quick by the cries of the crowd urging My death.

"I called to mind the sweet caresses of My Mother when she pressed Me to her heart... the toils of My adopted father, and the care with which he surrounded My life...

"I reviewed in spirit the benefits so liberally bestowed by Me on this ungrateful people... how I had given sight to the blind... health to the sick... healing to the lame... how I had fed the multitude in the desert... and even raised the dead to life... and see now to what a contemptible state I am reduced... more hated, too, than perhaps any man has ever been... condemned to death as an infamous thief... the multitude has demanded My death... Pilate has now given sentence. O all ye who love Me, attend and see the sufferings of My Heart!

p. 287 "After the betrayal in the Garden of Olives, Judas wandered away, a fugitive, a prey to the reproaches of his conscience which taxed him with the most execrable of sacrileges. And when he heard that I was condemned to death, he gave himself up to despair and hanged himself.

"Who can measure the deep and intense grief of My heart when I saw this soul so long taught by love... the recipient of My doctrine, one who had so often heard from My lips words of forgiveness for the most heinous crimes, finally throw himself into hell fire?

"Ah! Judas, why not throw yourself at My feet that I may forgive you too? If you are afraid to come near Me because of the raging mob that surrounds Me, or at least look at Me... My eyes will meet yours, for even now they are lovingly intent upon you.

"O all you who are steeped in sin, and who for a time more or less long have lived as wanderers and fugitives because of your crimes... if the offences of which you have been guilty have hardened and blinded your hearts... if to grant satisfaction to one or other of your passions you have sunk into evil ways... Ah! When the motives or accomplices of your sin have forsaken you, and you realize the state of your soul, O then, do not yield to despair! For as long as a breath of life remains a man may have recourse to mercy and ask for pardon.

"If you are still young, if already the scandals of your life have lowered you in the eyes of the world, do not be afraid... Even if there is reason to treat you as a criminal, to insult and cast you off... your God has no wish to see you fall into the flames of hell... On the contrary He ardently desires you to come to Him so that He may forgive you. If you dare not speak to Him, at least look at Him and let the sighs of your heart reach Him, and at once you will find His kind and fatherly hand stretched out to lead you to the springs of pardon and life.

"Should it happen that you have spent the greater part of your life in impiety and indifference, and that the sudden approach of the hour of death fills you with blinding despair... Ah! Do not let yourself be deceived, for there is still time for pardon. If only one second of life remains to you, in that one second you can buy back eternal life!

"If your whole life has been spent in ignorance and error... if you have been a cause of great evil to other men, to society at large, or to religion, and if through some set of circumstances you have come to realize that you have been deceived... do not allow yourself to be crushed by the weight of your sins and of the evil of which you have been the instrument, but with a soul penetrated with deep contrition throw yourself into an abyss of confidence, and hasten to Him who awaits your return only to pardon you.

"The case is the same for a soul that has been faithful to the observance of My law from childhood, but who has gradually cooled off into the tepid and unspiritual ways of an easy life. She has so to say forgotten her soul and its higher aspirations. God was asking of her greater efforts, but blinded by habitual failings, she has fallen into tepidity worse than actual sin, for her deaf and drowsy conscience neither feels remorse nor hears the voice of God.

"Then, perhaps, that soul awakens with a shock of realization: life appears to have been a failure, empty and useless for her salvation... She has lost innumerable graces, and the evil one, loath to lose her, makes the most of her distress, plunges her into discouragement, sadness and dejection... and finally casts her into fear and despair.

"O soul whom I love, pay no heed to this ruthless enemy... but as soon as possible have recourse to Me, and filled with deepest contrition implore My mercy and have no fear. I will forgive you. Take up again your life of fervour, and you will have back your lost merits, and My grace will never fail you.

"Finally, shall I speak to My chosen souls? Supposing that one has spent long years in the constant practice of the Rule and of her religious duties... a soul that I have favoured with My grace and instructed by My counsels... a soul long faithful to My voice and to the inspirations of grace ... and now this soul has cooled in her fervour on account of some petty passion... occasions of faults not avoided... some yielding to the claims of nature and a general relaxation of effort... and in consequence has fallen to a lower level... to a commonplace kind of life... then lastly, to give it its true name, tepidity. If, for one cause or another, you awake from this torpid state, the devil will instantly attack you in every way, jealous of a soul he hopes to claim. He will try to persuade you that it is too late, and that any effort is useless, he will accentuate your repugnance to make an avowal of your state of soul... he will, so to speak,

throttle you to prevent you from speaking and accepting the light... he will do his best to stifle trust and confidence in your soul.

'But listen rather to My voice, and let Me tell you how to act: As soon as your soul is touched by grace, and before the struggle has even begun, hasten to My Heart; beg of Me to let a drop of My Blood fall on your soul... Ah! hasten to My Heart... and be without fear for the past; all has been swallowed up in the abyss of My mercy, and My love is preparing new graces for you. The memory of your lapses will be an incentive to humility and a source of merit, and you cannot give Me a greater proof of affection than to count on My full pardon and to believe that your sins will never be as great as My mercy, which is infinite.

"Remain hidden, Josefa, in the abyss of My love, praying that souls may be filled with the same sentiments.

p. 243   " 'And now, Josefa, I will begin by discovering to you the thoughts that filled My Heart, while I was washing the feet of My Disciples.

" 'Mark how the whole twelve were gathered together, none excepted: John the beloved was there, and Judas who was so soon to deliver Me to My enemies. I will tell you why I willed to have them all assembled together and why I began by washing their feet.

" 'I gathered them all together because the moment had come for My Church to be manifested to the world, and for all the sheep to have but one Shepherd.

" 'It was My intention, also, to show souls that I never refuse grace even to those who are guilty of grave sin; nor do I separate them from the good whom I love with predilection. I keep them all in My Heart, that all may receive the help required by their state of soul...

" 'But how great was My sorrow to see in the person of My unhappy disciple Judas the throng of those who, though often gathered at My feet and washed with My Blood, would yet hasten to their eternal perdition.

" 'I would have these to understand that it is not the fact of being in sin that ought to keep them from Me., They must never think that there is no remedy for them, nor that they have forfeited for ever the love that once was theirs... No, poor souls, the God who has shed all His Blood for you has no such feelings for you!

" 'Come all of you to Me and fear not, for I love you all... I will wash you in my Blood and you shall be made whiter than snow. All your of-
p. 244   fences will be submerged in the waters in which I Myself shall wash you, nor shall anything whatsoever be able to tear from My Heart Its love for you.

" 'Josefa, let your soul be seized to-day by an ardent desire to see all souls, especially sinners, come and purify themselves in the waters of re-pentance... Let them give themselves up to thoughts of confidence, not fear, for I am a God of pity, ever ready to receive them into My Heart.' "

p. 246   "The hour of Redemption was at hand. My Heart could no longer restrain its love for mankind nor bear the thought of leaving them or-phans.

"So, to prove My tender love for them and in order to remain always with them till time has ceased to be, I resolved to become their food, their support, their life, their all. Could I but make known to all souls the loving sentiments with which My heart overflowed at My Last Supper, when I instituted the Sacrament of the Holy Eucharist...

"My glance ranged across the ages, and I saw the multitudes who would receive My Body and Blood, and all the good It would effect... how many hearts I saw that from Its contact would bud forth virginity!... and how many others that It would awaken to deeds of charity and zeal!... How many martyrs of love did I see... How many souls who had
p. 247   been enfeebled by sin and the violence of passion would come back to their allegiance and recover their spiritual energy by partaking of this Bread of the strong!...

p. 256   "Continue now to write for My souls: Tell them how they will find in the small white Host a perfect symbol of their vow of Chastity. For under the species of Bread and Wine the real presence of God lies concealed. Under this veil, I am there whole and entire, Body, Blood, Soul, and Divinity.

Good Friday
The Seven Words
30th and 31st March 1923

"Write all that you see"
(Our Lord to Josefa)

p. 306   From very early on Good Friday morning Our Lord united Josefa in with Himself in the scenes of the Crucifixion.

p. 307   "I saw Him a few moments later. He was fastened to the Cross, and it has been lifted up erect.

"'Peace has come to the world!... The Cross, hitherto an instrument of torture on which criminals were made to die, is changed into the light and peace of the world and the object of the most profound veneration.

p. 327   On Wednesday, 16th May, Josefa noted for the first time the apparition of the Cross.

"It was the Cross of Jesus," she wrote, "for I recognized it, having so often carried it. It was lit up as if a light from above was reflected on to it."

For several days the flaming Heart of Jesus and His Cross resplendent in light shone upon her path alternately, but in silence, and Her Master did not appear. On Whit-Sunday, 20th May 1923, the Cross thus lit up was before her during the whole time of her prayer; her eyes were fascinated by it and her love made more ardent, but she was nevertheless somewhat mystified.

p. 328   "Lord, why this Cross illuminated, but without Thee?" she queried.

During her thanksgiving, Jesus answered the question:

"Josefa, do you not know that I and the Cross are inseparable? If you meet Me, you meet the Cross, and when you find the Cross, it is I whom you have found. Whoever loves Me loves the Cross, and whoever loves the Cross loves Me. Only those who love the Cross and embrace it willingly for love of Me, will possess eternal life. The path of virtue and of holiness is composed of abnegation and suffering. Whoever generously accepts the Cross walks in true light, follows a straight and sure path, with no danger from steep inclines down which to slide, for there are none there.

"My Cross is the door of true life, that is why it is illuminated. And the soul that knows how to accept and love it, just as I have chosen it for her, will enter by it into the glory of life eternal.

"Do you now understand how precious the Cross is? Do not shun it... Love it, for it comes from Me, and I shall never leave you without strength to bear it. I bore it for love of you, will you not bear it for love of Me?

p. 334   After recording the words that she had heard, Josefa continued:

"Then I saw no one but Jesus alone, extending His hand, He said, with eyes raised to Heaven: 'May men adore the Father. May they love the Son. May they let themselves be possessed by the Holy Spirit, and may the Blessed Trinity abide in them'."

p. 335 "If a man devotes his life," He said, "to working either directly or indirectly for the salvation of souls, and reaches such a degree of detachment from self that without neglecting his own perfection he leaves to others the merit of his actions, prayers and sufferings... that man draws down abundant graces on the world... he himself reaches a high degree of sanctity, far higher than he would have attained had he sought only his own advancement."

p. 351 AN APPEAL TO THE WHOLE WORLD

Do Men Know?
10th-14th June 1923

"All My longing is to set hearts on fire... to set the whole world on fire"
(Our Lord to Josefa, 12th June 1923)

The time has now come, when according to the divine will, Josefa was to transmit the desires of the Sacred Heart to the Bishop of Poitiers.

p. 352 A few minutes later Our Lord rejoined her in her cell. "I am now about to tell you, Josefa, the first thing that you are to tell the Bishop. Kiss the ground!"

She renewed her vows and prostrated herself at His feet. Then Jesus began to speak and Josefa wrote:

"I am *Love!* My Heart can no longer contain its devouring flames. I love souls so dearly that I have sacrificed My life for them.

p. 353 "This is what I wish all to know. I will teach sinners that the mercy of My Heart is inexhaustible. Let the callous and indifferent know that My Heart is a fire which will enkindle them, because I love them. To devout and saintly souls I would be the Way, that making great strides in perfection, they may safely reach the harbour of eternal beatitude. Lastly, of consecrated souls, priests and religious, My elect and chosen ones, I ask, once more, all their love and that they should not doubt mine, but above all that they should trust Me and never doubt My mercy. It is so easy to trust completely in My Heart!"

p. 354 "I want to forgive. I want to reign over souls and pardon all nations. I want to rule souls, nations, the whole world. My peace must be extended over the entire universe, but in a special way over this dear country where devotion to My Heart first took root… O that I might be its peace, its life, its King. I am Wisdom and Beatitude! I am Love and Mercy! I am Peace, I shall reign! I will shower My mercies on the world to wipe out its ingratitude. To make reparation for its crimes, I will choose victims who will obtain pardon… for there are in the world many whose desire is to please Me… and there are moreover generous souls who will sacrifice everything they possess, that I may use them according to My will and good pleasure.

"My reign will be the one of peace and love and I shall inaugurate it by compassion on all: such is the end I have in view and this is the great work of My love."

Then with divinest condescension Our Lord explained to Josefa, that she might tell the Bishop the reasons that caused His choice of the Society of the Sacred Heart to be the intermediary to the world of His designs. "It is *founded* on love, its *end* is love, its *life* is love… and what is love but My Heart?"

Thus did Our Lord outline in a few brief words the bond that was to exist between His work and the Society.

"As for you," He said to Josefa, "I have chosen you as a useless and incapable being, so that it may be clearly I who speak, who ask, who act.

"My appeal is addressed to all: to those consecrated in religion and to those living in the world, to the good and to sinners, to the learned and to the illiterate, to those in authority and to those who obey. To each of them I come to say: if you seek happiness you will find it in Me. If riches, I am infinite Wealth. If you desire peace, in Me alone is peace to be found. I am Mercy and Love! and I must be sovereign King…"

Then, turning to Josefa, who was kneeling and had just transcribed the last burning words of her Master: "This is what you will first give the Bishop to read."

p. 356 So now once again Jesus spoke to the world in a parable, this time to make known the vastness of His all-embracing love.

"So now, Josefa, write.

"A father had an only son.

"They were rich and powerful, served by devoted retainers, and surrounded by all that makes for honour, comfort and pleasure in life, and nothing, neither person nor thing, was wanting to their good fortune. The son was all in all to the father, and the father to the son, and each found in the other perfect contentment, though not so as to exclude others, for such noble and generous hearts felt sympathy for anyone in distress, however slight it might be.

"Now it came to pass that one of the servants of this good master fell ill, and as the danger increased, the only hope of saving his life lay in the application of powerful remedies and most careful nursing.

"But this servant lay at his poor and lonely home. At which the master felt alarm, for if left deserted, the man would certainly die. What was to be done? True, a fellow servant could be sent to minister to him; but such service, done for gain rather than love, gave no assurance against possible neglect.

"So, moved with compassion, the master called his son, and told him of his anxiety. He explained how near death the poor man was, and that the most unremitting care alone could save him.

"Like father, like son! The offer to go himself to succour the dying man is made at once. He will spare neither trouble, fatigue nor night watches until the servant's health is fully re-established.

p. 357 "The father accepts his son's offer, and willingly allows him to take on the likeness of a servant, that he may serve him who is his slave.

"Many months go by, months of anxious watching by the sickbed, till at length health is restored, for nothing has been spared that could not only cure his sickness, but also ensure his complete well-being. And what of the servant? With a heart overflowing with gratitude, he asks what *he* can do in return for such marvelous charity.

" 'Go,' said the son, 'seek out my father and with restored health offer yourself to become his most faithful servant in return for his liberality.'

"Overwhelmed by his obligations, the man stands in humble gratitude before his benefactor and proffers his services gratis, for ever. What need has he of remuneration from such a master, who has treated him not as a servant, but as a son.

"This parable is but a pale image of the love I bear to mankind, and of the loving return I look for from them. I will explain it so that all men may know My Heart.

p. 358 Our Lord then explained the parable of yesterday:

"God created man out of pure love. He placed him on the earth in circumstances that ensured his happiness until the day of eternal bliss should dawn for him. But to have a right to such felicity he is bound to keep the sweet and wise laws laid down by His Maker.

"Man, unfaithful to this law, fell grievously sick; sin was committed by our first parents, and all mankind, their descendants, contracted this guilt and lost their right to the perfect beatitude promised them by God; and pain, suffering and death became henceforth their lot.

"Now God, in perfect bliss, has no need of man or of his services. He is sufficient unto himself. Infinite is His glory and nothing can diminish it.

"Infinite in power, He is also infinite in goodness; hence He will not allow man, created out of love, to perish; instead, he met the grave evil of sin with a remedy infinite in price: one of the divine Persons of the Blessed Trinity, assuming human nature, will repair in a godlike manner the evil of the Fall.

p. 359 "The Father gives His Son, the Son sacrifices His glory. He comes to earth not as an all-powerful Lord and Master, but in poverty as a servant and as a child.

"The life He led on earth is known to you all.

"You know how from the first moment of the Incarnation I submitted to all human afflictions. In My childhood I endured cold, hunger, poverty, and persecution.

"In My life of labour, how often humiliation and contempt were meted out to the carpenter's son. How often after a hard day's work we, My foster-father and I, found that we had earned hardly sufficient to support us... and this I continued for thirty long years.

"Then, forgoing the sweet company of My Mother, I devoted Myself to the task of making My heavenly Father known. I went about teaching men that God is Love.

"I went about doing good to bodies as well as souls: to the sick I gave back their health; the dead I raised to life; and to souls?... Ah! to souls I restored liberty... that liberty which they had lost through sin, and I opened to them the gates of their everlasting home–Heaven.

"Then came the hour when to win salvation for them the Son of God willed to surrender life itself.

"And how did He die?... Was He surrounded by friends?... Acclaimed as a benefactor?... Beloved ones, you know that the son of God did not will to die thus. He who had preached nothing but love was the victim of hatred... He who had brought peace to the world was treated most cruelly... He who came to bring men freedom was imprisoned, bound, ill-used, calumniated, and finally died on a cross between two thieves... condemned, abandoned, abject and despoiled of everything.

"It was thus he surrendered Himself for man's salvation. It was thus He accomplished the work for which He had voluntarily left His Father's glory. Man was sick and wounded, and the Son of God came down to him. He not only restored fallen man to life, but earned for him both strength and power to acquire in this life the treasures of eternal beatitude.

"And what was man's response?

"Did he, like the grateful servant, offer his ministrations gratis and renounce any other but His Master's interests?...

"Let us consider and distinguish... for there are different ways in p. 360 which a response has been made by man.

"But this is enough for to-day. Remain in My peace, Josefa, and do not forget that you are My victim. Love, and leave all the rest to Me."

The Response made by Mankind
15th-19th June 1923

Then He explained to Josefa the different responses of mankind to God's offer of love.

"Some have truly known Me, and urged by love, have ardently desired to make an entire sacrifice of themselves to My service, which is that of My Father. They begged to be told the greatest thing they could do for Him, and My Father answered thus: 'Leave your home, give up our possessions, and having surrendered *self*, come, follow Me, and do whatever I tell you.'

"Others, moved by all that the Son of God had done for their salvation, offered themselves to Him, endeavouring with good will to make a return for His goodness, by working for His interests, but without entire renunciation of their own. To these My Father says: 'Observe the law which the Lord your God has given you. Keep His commandments, and erring neither to right nor left, live in the peace which belongs to faithful servants.'

"There are others again who have little understanding of God's great love, yet they have an upright will and live under the law, but without love.

"These servants have not volunteered to carry out all God's orders… yet a slight indication of His Will is often enough to enlist their service, since they are men of good will.

"There are yet others who submit to their God, not so much through love as through self-interest, and only fulfill the law as far as is necessary to ensure their salvation.

"Yet, do all men offer God their service? Are there any who through ignorance of the great love of which they are the object, make no response to all that the Son of God has suffered for them?

"Alas!... there are many who know and despise it... but a far greater number are entirely ignorant of it..."

For each of these Jesus Christ has a word of love:

"I will speak in the first place to those who do not know Me:

"My sons, who from infancy have lived apart from your Father, come, I will tell you why you do not know me... for once you realize the affection I bear you, you will not resist My love.

"It is often the case that those brought up far from their parents have little affection for them; but when by chance the sweet love of father or mother is manifested to them, there awakens a keener appreciation of this warm devotion than is found in those who have never left home.

"To you, who not only do not love, but hate and persecute Me, I say: 'Why this hatred?.... What have I done to deserve persecution at your hands?... There are many who have never asked themselves this question. To-day when I ask it, they will perhaps say: 'We do not know' Behold, I will answer for you: 'If from childhood you have never known Me, it is because no one has ever taught you about Me; and as you grew up, nature also was developing in your love of pleasure and enjoyment, a longing for wealth and freedom. Then came the day when first you heard of Me, and how to live according to My will; that to do so you must love and bear with your neighbour, respect his rights and his goods and gain a mastery of your own nature, in a word, live subject to a law. Hitherto, subject only to your own natural inclinations, if not to your passions, not knowing even of what law there was question, to you I say, is it to be wondered at that you should protest, should wish to enjoy life, to be free, and to be a law unto yourself?

"In this lies the beginning of your hatred and persecution of Me. But I, your Father, love you, and even as I see your blind revolt, My Heart is filled with tenderness for you.

"So the years in which you led this life sped by, and they were, perhaps, many...

"To-day I can no longer restrain My love for you, and the sight of you at war with your best friend compels Me to enlighten you as to who I am.

"Dearly loved son, I am *Jesus*, which name signifies *Saviour*! why else are My hands transfixed with nails which fasten them to a cross? On it, for love of you, I died. My feet are wounded, My Heart wide open, riven by the lance after death... Thus do I stand before you that you may know who I am and what My law is. But do not fear–My law is one of love... and in knowing Me you will find peace and joy. It is sad to live as an orphan: come, My sons, come to your Father.

p. 371 "As God, He demands of you the accomplishment of His divine law.

"As your Father, He asks you to accept His commandments in a spirit of filial piety.

"Thus, when you have spent a week in the pursuit of work, business or sport, He claims but one half-hour, that you may fulfil your Sunday duty. Is this excessive?

"Go then to your Father's House, where day and night He awaits your coming, and as Sundays and Holidays recur, give Him the homage of this half hour by assisting at the Mystery of Love and Mercy, that is, Holy Mass.

"Tell Him about everything: about your families, your children, your business, your desires... Lay at His feet your sorrows, difficulties and sufferings... believe in the interest and love with which He listens to your prayer.

"You may perhaps say to Me: 'I have not entered a church for so many years that I have forgotten how to hear Mass.' Do not be afraid on that account... Come, spend this half-hour with Me; your conscience will tell you what to do, and be docile to its voice... Open your soul wide to grace, and it will inspire you... Gradually it will teach you how to act in a given circumstance, how to treat with your family, what to do in regard to your business... how to bring up your children, love those who depend on you, and honour those in authority over you... It may make you feel that such and such a concern must be given up, such a friendship relinquished, or such a meeting avoided... Again, it may tell you that you are hating a certain person quite unreasonably; or it may put it into your mind to sever your connection with some person you feel drawn to and whose advice is doing you harm. Only give grace a chance, and gradually its power will grow stronger in you, for just as evil increases insensibly, once it is given in to, so will each new grace prepare your soul for a still greater one. If to-day you listen to My voice and let grace act, to-morrow its influence will be stronger and so steadily increase as time goes on; light will grow in your soul, peace envelop you, and the reward will be eternal bliss.

"Man was not created to live for ever here below. He was made for eternity… If then he is immortal, he should live, not for the passing things of time, but for that which will never die.

"Youth, wealth, wisdom, human glory, all that is nothing, it will all end with this life; God only will endure for ever.

"The world is full of hate, races are in perpetual conflict with one another, so are nations, and even individuals, and all this is due to the decay of faith. Only let faith reign once more over the world and peace and charity will return to it.

"Faith in no way impedes civilization and progress. The more it is rooted in individuals and peoples, the more wisdom and learning increase, for God is infinite in wisdom and knowledge. But whenever faith is completely lacking, peace, civilization and true progress likewise vanish… for God is not in war… and in their place come enmities, clash of opinions, class wars, and within man himself, rebellion of passions against duty. All that is noble in humanity is exchanged for revolt, insubordination and warfare…

"Let yourselves be convinced by faith and you will be great. Let yourselves be ruled by faith, and you will be free; live by faith, and you will escape eternal death."

Such were the last words of Christ's *Message* to the world.

Then He looked down at Josefa and said: "Adieu. You know that I expect reparation and love from you all. Love is proved by deeds, so let all your works prove your love. Be messengers of love in things great and small. Do all for love. Live by love."

He vanished.

180   + During Advent, a great yearning for God arose in my soul. My spirit rushed toward God with all its might. During that time, the Lord gave me much light to know His attributes.

The first attribute which the Lord gave me to know is His holiness. His holiness is so great that all the Powers and Virtues tremble before Him. The pure spirits veil their faces and lose themselves in unending adoration, and with one single word they express the highest form of adoration; that is – Holy... The holiness of God is poured out upon the Church of God and upon every living soul in it, but not in the same degree. There are souls who are completely penetrated by God, and there are those who are barely alive.

The second kind of knowledge which the Lord granted me concerns His justice. His justice is so great and penetrating that it reaches deep into the heart of things, and all things stand before Him in naked truth, and nothing can withstand Him.

The third attribute is love and mercy. And I understood that the greatest attribute is love and mercy. It unites the creature with the Creator. This immense love and abyss of mercy are made known in the Incarnation of the Word and in the Redemption [of humanity], and it is here that I saw this as the greatest of all God's attributes.

477   Silence is a sword in the spiritual struggle. A talkative soul will never attain sanctity. The sword of silence will cut off everything that would like to cling to the soul. We are sensitive to words and quickly want to answer back, without taking any regard as to whether it is God's will that we should speak. A silent soul is strong; no adversities will harm it if it perseveres in silence. The silent (**198**) soul is capable of attaining the closest union with God. It lives almost always under the inspiration of the Holy Spirit. God works in a silent soul without hindrance.

732   + The great majesty of God which pervaded me today and still pervades me awoke in me a great fear, but a fear filled with respect, and not the fear of a slave, which is quite different from the fear of respect. This fear animated by respect arose in my heart today because of love and the knowledge of the greatness of God, and that is a great joy to the soul. The soul trembles before the smallest offense against God; but that does not trouble or darken its happiness. There, where love is in charge, all is well.

803   My room is next to the men's ward. I didn't know that men were such chatterboxes. From morning till late at night, there is talk about various subjects. The women's ward is much quieter. It is women who are always blamed for this; but I have had occasion to be convinced that the opposite is true. It is very difficult for me to concentrate on my prayer in the midst of these jokes and this laughter. They do not disturb me when the grace of God takes complete possession of me, (201) because then I do not know what is going on around me.

818   December 16, [1936]. I have offered this day for Russia. I have offered all my sufferings and prayers for that poor country. After Holy Communion, Jesus said to me, **I cannot suffer that country any longer. Do not tie my hands, My daughter. (209)** I understood that if it had not been for the prayers of souls that are pleasing to God, that whole nation would have already been reduced to nothingness. Oh, how I suffer for that nation which has banished God from its borders!

873   (**246**) January 8. On Friday morning, as I was going to the chapel to attend Holy Mass, I suddenly saw a huge juniper tree on the pavement and in it a horrible cat who, looking angrily at me, blocked my way to the chapel. One whisper of the name of Jesus dissipated all that. I offered the whole day for dying sinners. During Holy Mass, I felt the closeness of the Lord in a special way. After Holy Communion, I turned my gaze with trust toward the Lord and told him, "Jesus, I so much desire to tell you something." And the Lord looked at me with love and said, **And what is it that you desire to tell Me?**

    "Jesus, I beg You, by the inconceivable power of Your mercy, that all the souls who will die today escape the fire of hell, even if they have been the greatest sinners. Today is Friday, the memorial of Your bitter agony on the Cross; because Your mercy is inconceivable, the Angels will not be surprised at this." Jesus pressed me to His Heart and said, **My beloved (247) daughter, you have come to know well the depths of My mercy. I will do what you ask, but unite yourself continually with My agonizing Heart and make reparation to My justice. Know that you have asked Me for a great thing, but I see that this was dictated by your pure love for Me; that is why I am complying with your requests.**

888 Silence is so powerful a language that it reaches the throne of the living God. Silence is His language, though secret, yet living and powerful.

897 (**262**) January 27, 1937. I feel considerable improvement in my health. Jesus is bringing me from the gates of death to life, because there was so little left but for me to die, and lo, the Lord grants me the fullness of life. Although I am still to remain in the sanatorium, I am almost completely well. I see that the will of God has not yet been fulfilled in me, and that is why I must live, for I know that if I fulfill everything the Lord has planned for me in this world, He will not leave me in exile any longer, for heaven is my home. But before we go to our Homeland, we must fulfill the will of God on earth; that is, trials and struggles must run their full course in us.

911 On one occasion, God's presence pervaded my whole being, and my mind was mysteriously enlightened in respect to His Essence. He allowed me to understand His interior life. In spirit, I saw the Three Divine Persons, but Their Essence was One. He is One, and One only, but in Three Persons; none of Them is either greater or smaller; there is no difference in either beauty or sanctity, for They are One. They are absolutely One. His Love transported me into this knowledge and united me with Himself. When I was united to One, I was equally united in the Second and to the Third in such a way that when we are united with One, by that very fact, we are equally united to the two persons in the same way as with the One. Their will is One, one God, though in Three Persons. When One of the Three persons communicates with a soul, (**269**) by the power of that one will, it finds itself united with the Three Persons and is inundated in the happiness flowing from the Most Holy Trinity, the same happiness that nourishes the saints. This same happiness that streams from the Most Holy Trinity makes all creation happy; from it springs that life which vivifies and bestows all life which takes its beginning from Him. In these moments, my soul experienced such great divine delights that I find this difficult to express.

990 I know well, O Lord, that You have no need of our works; You demand love. Love, love and once again, love of God – there is nothing greater in heaven or on earth. The greatest greatness is to love God; true greatness is in loving God; real wisdom is to love God. All that is great and beautiful is in God; there is no beauty or greatness outside of Him. O you sages of the world and you great minds, recognize that true greatness is in loving God! Oh, how astonished I am that some people deceive themselves, saying: There is no eternity!

1008   March 1, 1937. The Lord gave me to know how displeased He is with a talkative soul. **I find no rest in such a soul. The constant din tires Me, and in the midst of it the soul cannot discern My voice.**

1029   The doctor did not allow me to go to the chapel to attend the Passion Service, although I had a great desire for it; however, I prayed in my own room. Suddenly I heard the bell in the next room, and I went in and rendered a service to a seriously sick person. (**8**) When I returned to my room, I suddenly saw the Lord Jesus, who said, **My daughter, you gave Me greater pleasure by rendering Me that service than if you had prayed for a long time.** I answered, "But it was not to You, Jesus, but to that patient that I rendered this service." And the Lord answered me, **Yes, My daughter, but whatever you do for your neighbor, you do for Me.**

1090   And this happened on the last of my novena to the Holy Spirit. After this return to health, I found myself united with the Lord Jesus in a purely spiritual way. Jesus gave me strong assurances; that is, He confirmed me in respect to His demands. I remained close to the Lord Jesus all that day and talked with Him about the details concerning that congregation.

(**24**) Jesus infused my soul with power and courage to act. Now I understand that if the Lord demands something of a soul, He gives it the means to carry it out, and through grace he makes it capable of doing this. So, even if the soul be utterly miserable, at the Lord's command it can undertake things beyond its expectation, because this is the sign by which it can be known that the Lord is with that soul: if God's power and strength, which make the soul courageous and valiant, is manifest within it. As for myself, I am always at first a bit frightened at the Lord's greatness, but afterwards my soul is filled with profound peace which nothing can disturb, as well as an inner strength to do what the Lord is demanding at that particular moment....

1107   Today during meditation, God gave me inner light and the understanding as to what sanctity is and of what it consists. Although I have heard these things many times in conferences, the soul understands them in a different way when it comes to know of them through the light of God which illumines it.

Neither graces, nor revelations, nor raptures, nor gifts granted to a soul make it perfect, but rather the intimate union of the soul with God. These gifts are merely ornaments of the soul, but constitute neither its essence nor its perfection. My sanctity and perfection consist in the close union of my will with the will of God. God never violates our free will. It is up to us whether we want to receive God's grace or not. It is up to us whether we will cooperate with it or waste it.

1151   (**41**)   + When pain overwhelms my soul,
And the horizon darkens like night,
And the heart is torn with the torment of suffering,
Jesus Crucified, You are my strength.

    When the soul, dimmed with pain,
    Exerts itself in battle without respite,
    And the heart is in agony and torment,
    Jesus Crucified, You are the hope of my salvation.

And so the days pass,
As the soul bathes in a sea of bitterness,
And the heart dissolves in tears,
Jesus Crucified, You shine for me like the dawn.

    And when the cup of bitterness brims over,
    And all things conspire against her,
    And the soul goes down to the Garden of Olives,
    Jesus Crucified, in You is my defense.

When the soul, conscious of its innocence,
Accepts these dispensations from God,
The heart can then repay hurts with love,
Jesus Crucified, transform my weakness into omnipotence.

1160   (**44**) When once I asked the Lord Jesus how He could tolerate so many sins and crimes and not punish them, the Lord answered me, **I have eternity for punishing** [these], **and so I am prolonging the time of mercy for the sake of** [sinners]. **But woe to them if they do not recognize this time of My visitation. My daughter, secretary of My mercy, your duty is not only to write about and proclaim My mercy, but also to beg for this grace for them, so that they too many glorify My mercy.**

1170   June 30, 1937. Today, the Lord said to me, **I have wanted to exalt this Congregation many times, but I am unable to do so because of its pride. Know, My daughter, that I do not grant My graces to proud souls, and I even take away from them the graces I have granted.**

1181   When I was close to the Lord, He said to me, **Why are you afraid to begin the work which I have commanded you to carry out?** I answered, "Why do You leave me on my own at such times, Jesus, and why do I not feel Your presence?" **My daughter, even though you do not perceive Me in the most secret depths of your heart, you still cannot say that I am not there. I only remove from you the awareness of My presence, and that should not be an obstacle to the carrying out of My will. I do this to achieve My unfathomable ends, which you will know of later on.**

My daughter, know without doubt, and once and for all, that only mortal sin drives me out of a soul, and nothing else.

1188   I often pray for Poland, but I see that God is very angry with it because of its ingratitude.[201] I exert all the strength of my soul to defend it. I constantly remind God of the promises of His mercy. When I see His anger, I throw myself trustingly into the abyss of His mercy, and I plunge all Poland in it, and then he cannot use His justice. My country, how much you cost me! There is no day in which I do not pray for you.

1232   O sweet Mother of God,
        I model my life on You;
        You are for me the bright dawn;
        In You I lose myself, enraptured.

            O Mother, Immaculate Virgin,
            In You the divine ray is reflected,
            Midst storms, 'tis You who teach me to love the Lord,
            O my shield and defense from the foe.

        Cracow, August 10, 1937.

        O Sacred Host, fountain of divine sweetness,
        You give strength to my soul;
        O You are the Omnipotent One, who took flesh of the Virgin,
        You come to my heart, in secret,
        Beyond reach of the groping senses.

1240   (**6**) The Lord Jesus greatly protects His representatives on earth. How closely He is united with them; and He orders me to give priority to their opinion over His. I have come to know the great intimacy which exists between Jesus and the priest. Jesus defends whatever the priest says, and often complies with his wishes, and sometimes makes His own relationship with a soul depend on the priest's advice. O Jesus, through a special grace, I have come to know very clearly to what extent You have shared Your power and mystery with them, more so than with the Angels. I rejoice in this, for it is all for my good.

1262   September 3. First Friday of the month. During Holy Mass, I became united with God. Jesus gave me to know that even the smallest thing does not happen on earth without His will. After having seen this, my soul entered into an unusual repose; I found myself completely at peace as to the work in its full extent. God can deal with me as He pleases, and I will bless Him for everything.

1276   September 16, 1937. I wanted very much to make a Holy Hour before the Blessed Sacrament today, but God's will was otherwise. At eight o'clock I was seized with such violent pains that (**31**) I had to go to bed at once. I was convulsed with pain for three hours; that is, until eleven o'clock at night. No medicine had any effect on me, and whatever I swallowed I threw up. At times, the pains caused me to lose consciousness. Jesus had me realize that in this way I took part in His Agony in the Garden, and that He Himself allowed these sufferings in order to offer reparation to God for the souls murdered in the wombs of wicked mothers. I have gone through these sufferings three times now. They always start at eight o'clock in the evening and last until eleven. No medicine can lessen these sufferings. When eleven o'clock comes, they cease by themselves, and I fall asleep at that moment. The following day, I feel very weak.

This happened to me for the first time when I was at the sanatorium. The doctors couldn't get to the bottom of it, and no injection or medicine helped me at all (**32**) nor did I myself have any idea of what the sufferings were about. I told the doctor that never before in my life had I experienced such sufferings, and he declared he did not know what sort of pains they are. But now I understand the nature of these pains, because the Lord Himself has made this known to me....Yet when I think that I may perhaps suffer in this way again, I tremble. But I don't know whether I'll ever again suffer in this way; I leave that to God. What it pleases God to send, I will accept with submission and love. If only I could save even one soul from murder by means of these sufferings!

1288   September 19, [1937]. Today, the Lord told me, **My daughter, write that it pains Me very much when religious souls receive the Sacrament of Love merely out of habit, as if they did not distinguish this food. I find neither faith nor love in their hearts. I go to such souls with great reluctance. It would be better if they did not receive Me.**

1322   The barque of my life sails along
Amid darkness and shadows of night,
And I see no shore;
I am sailing the high seas.

    The slightest storm would drown me,
Engulfing my boat in the swirling depths,
If You Yourself did not watch over me, O God,
At each instant and moment of my life.

Amid the roaring waves
I sail peacefully, trustingly,
And gaze like a child into the distance without fear,
Because You, O Jesus, are my Light.

    Dread and terror is all about me,
But within my soul is peace more profound than the depths of
the sea,
For he who is with You, O Lord, will not perish;
Of this Your love assures me, O God.

Though a host of dangers surround me,
None of them do I fear, for I fix my gaze on the starry sky,
And I sail along bravely and merrily,
As becomes a pure heart.

    And if the ship of my life sails so peacefully,
This is due to but one thing above all:
You are my helmsman, O God,
This I confess with utmost humility.

1354   When I hesitate on how to act in some situations, I always ask Love. It advises best.

1407   When I was receiving Holy Communion today, I noticed in the cup a Living Host, which the priest gave to me. When I returned to my place I asked the Lord, "Why was one Host alive, since You are equally alive under each of the species?" The Lord answered me, **That is so. I am the same under each of the species, but not every soul receives Me with the same living faith as you do, My daughter, and therefore I cannot act in their souls as I do in yours.**

1409   + Today the Lord Jesus is giving me an awareness of Himself and of His most tender love and care for me. He is bringing me to understand deeply how everything depends on His will, and how he allows certain difficulties precisely for our merit, so that our fidelity might be clearly manifest. And through this, I have been given strength for suffering and self-denial.

1420   When I steeped myself in prayer, I was transported in spirit to the chapel, where I saw the Lord Jesus, exposed in the monstrance. In place of the monstrance, I saw the glorious face of the Lord, and He said to me, **What you see in reality, these souls see through faith. Oh, how pleasing to Me is their great faith! You see, although there appears to be no trace of life in Me, in reality it is present in its fullness in each and every Host. But for Me to be able to act upon a soul, the soul must have faith. O how pleasing to me is living faith!**

1443   (**58**) My soul was languishing with joy. But toward the end of the Mass, I felt so weak that I had to leave the chapel and go to my cell, as I felt unable to take part in the community tea. But my joy throughout the whole Christmas Season was immense, because my soul was unceasingly united with the Lord. I have come to know that every soul would like to have divine comforts, but is by no means willing to forsake human comforts, whereas these two things cannot be reconciled.

1448   **Write, speak of My mercy. Tell souls where they are to look for solace; that is, in the Tribunal of Mercy** [the Sacrament of Reconciliation] **There the greatest miracles take place** [and] **are incessantly repeated. To avail oneself of this miracle, it is not necessary to go on a great pilgrimage or to carry out some external ceremony; it suffices to come with faith to the feet of My representative and to reveal to him one's misery, and the miracle of Divine Mercy will be fully demonstrated. Were a soul like a decaying corpse so that from a human standpoint, there would be no** [hope of] **restoration and everything would already be lost, it is not so with God. The miracle of Divine Mercy restores that soul in full. Oh, how miserable are those who do not take advantage of the miracle of God's mercy! You will call out in vain, but it will be too late.**

1487   Soul: One more thing, Lord. What should I do when I am ignored and rejected by people, especially by those on whom I have a right to count in times of greatest need?

Jesus: **My child, make the resolution never to rely on people. Entrust yourself completely to My will saying, "Not as I want, but according to Your will, O God, let be done unto me." These words, spoken from the depths of one's heart, can raise a soul to the summit of sanctity in a short time. In such a soul I delight. Such a soul gives Me glory. Such a soul fills heaven with the fragrance of her virtue. But understand that the strength by which you bear sufferings comes from frequent Communions. So approach this fountain of mercy often, to draw with the vessel of trust whatever you need.**

1507   All grace flows from mercy, and the last hour abounds with mercy for us. Let no one doubt concerning the goodness of God; even if a person's sins were as dark as night, God's mercy is stronger than our misery. One thing alone is necessary: that the sinner set ajar the door of his heart, be it ever so little, to let in a ray of God's merciful grace, and then God will do the rest. But poor is the soul who has shut the door on God's mercy, even at the last hour. It was just such souls who plunged Jesus into deadly sorrow in the Garden of Olives; indeed, it was from His Most Merciful Heart that divine mercy flowed out.

1578   **Let souls who are striving for perfection particularly adore My mercy, because the abundance of graces which I grant them flows from My mercy. I desire that these souls distinguish themselves by boundless trust in My mercy. I myself will attend to the sanctification of such souls. I will provide them with everything they will need to attain sanctity. The graces of My mercy are drawn by means of one vessel only, and that is – trust. The more a soul trust, the more it will receive. Souls that trust boundlessly are a great comfort to Me, because I pour all the treasures of My graces into them. I rejoice that they ask for much, because it is My desire to give much, very much. On the other hand, I am sad when souls ask for little, when they narrow their hearts.**

1588   Today I heard the words: **in the Old Covenant I sent prophets wielding thunderbolts to My people. Today I am sending you with My mercy to the people of the whole world. I do not want to punish aching mankind, but I desire to heal it, pressing it to My Merciful Heart. I use punishment when they themselves force Me to do so; My hand is reluctant to take hold of the sword of justice. Before the Day of Justice I am sending the Day of Mercy.** I replied, "O my Jesus, speak to souls Yourself, because my words are insignificant."

1628   During Holy Mass, I saw Jesus stretched out on the Cross, and he said to me, **My pupil, have great love for those who cause you suffering. Do good to those who hate you.** I answered, "O my Master, You see very well that I feel no love for them, and that troubles me." Jesus answered, **It is not always within your power to control your feelings. You will recognize that you have love, if, after having experienced annoyance and contradiction, you do not lose your peace, but pray for those who have made you suffer and wish them well.** When I returned [...]

J. M. J.

O truth, O thorny life,
In order to pass through you victoriously
It is necessary to lean on You, O Christ,
And to be always close to You.

I would not know how to suffer without You, O Christ,
Of myself I would not be able to brave adversities.
Alone, I would not have the courage to drink from Your cup;
But You, Lord, are always with me, and You lead me along mysterious paths.

A weak child, I have begun the battle in Your Name.
I have fought bravely, though often without success,
(**42**) And I know that my efforts have pleased You,
And I know that it is the effort alone which You eternally reward.

O truth, O life-and-death struggle,
When I rose to do battle, an inexperienced knight,
I felt I had a knight's blood, though still a child,
And therefore, O Christ, I needed Your help and protection.

My heart will not rest from its efforts and struggle
Until You Yourself call me from the field of battle.

I will stand before You, not to receive a reward,
But to be drowned in You, in peace forever.

1695 Then I heard the words, **I am glad you behaved like My true daughter. Be always merciful as I am merciful. Love everyone out of love for Me, even your greatest enemies, so that My mercy may be fully reflected (69) in your heart.**

1698 (**70**) I often attend upon the dying and through entreaties obtain for them trust in God's mercy, and I implore God for an abundance of divine grace, which is always victorious. God's mercy sometimes touches the sinner at the last moment in a wondrous and mysterious way. Outwardly, it seems as if everything were lost, but it is not so. The soul, illumined by a ray of God's powerful final grace, turns to God in the last moment with such a power of love that, in an instant, it receives from God forgiveness of sin and punishment, while outwardly it shows no sign either of repentance or of contrition, because souls [at that stage] no longer react to external things. Oh, how beyond comprehension is God's mercy! But – horror! – there are also souls who voluntarily and consciously reject and scorn this grace! Although a person is at the point of death, the merciful God gives the soul that interior vivid moment, so that if the soul is willing, it has the possibility of returning to God. But sometimes, the obduracy (**71**) in souls is so great that consciously they choose hell; they [thus] make useless all the prayers that other souls offer to God for them and even the efforts of God Himself...

1710   **(80)** May 26, [1938 – Feast of the Ascension]. Today I accompanied the Lord Jesus as He ascended into heaven. It was about noon. I was overcome by a great longing for God. It is a strange thing, the more I felt God's presence, the more ardently I desired Him. Then I saw myself in the midst of a huge crowd of disciples and apostles, together with the Mother of God. Jesus was telling them to...**Go out into the whole world and teach in My name.** He stretched out His hands and blessed them and disappeared in a cloud. I saw the longing of Our Lady. Her soul yearned for Jesus with the whole force of Her love. But She was so peaceful and so united to the will of God that there was not a stir in Her heart but for what God wanted.

1728   **(90) Write: I am Thrice Holy, and I detest the smallest sin. I cannot love a soul which is stained with sin; but when it repents, there is no limit to My generosity toward it. My mercy embraces and justifies it. With My mercy, I pursue sinners along all their paths, and My Heart rejoices when they return to Me. I forget the bitterness with which they fed My Heart and rejoice at their return.**

    Tell sinners that no one shall escape My Hand; if they run away from My Merciful Heart, they will fall into My Just Hands. Tell sinners that I am always waiting for them, that I listen intently to the beating of their heart...when will it beat for Me? Write, that I am speaking to them through their remorse of conscience, through the failures and sufferings, through thunderstorms, through the voice of the Church. And if they bring all My graces to naught, I begin to be angry (91) with them, leaving them alone and giving them what they want.

1732   As I was praying for Poland, I heart the words: **I bear a special love for Poland, and if she will be obedient to My will, I will exalt her in might and holiness. From her will come forth the spark that will prepare the world for My final coming.**

1768   **My daughter, in this meditation, consider the love of neighbor. Is your love for your neighbor guided by My love? Do you pray for your enemies? Do you wish well to those who have, in one way or another, caused you sorrow or offended you?**

    Know that whatever good (125) you do to any soul, I accept it as if you had done it to Me.

God talks to us through His Divine Writings as in the *Bible* and these two books.
We talk to God through our prayers.
How much fun hanging out with the Creator of the Universe.

My friend Rick O'Hara once told me the letters of the word *Bible* stand for **b**asic
instruction **b**efore **l**eaving **e**arth. For a more intimate relationship with
God the Father/God the Son/God the Holy Spirit, read the *Bible*,
read *The Way of Divine Love*, and read *Divine Mercy in My Soul*.

Bible	any local church	or book store
The Way of Divine Love	TAN Books stopped printing	the Holy Spirit will help you find a copy
Divine Mercy in My Soul	marian.org	or call 800-462-742

I look forward to meeting you on the other side. (heaven)

Sincerely in Christ,

Mark W. Bass

Mark W. Bass

Mark W. Bass

I was born in St. Louis, Missouri
and raised in Columbus, Ohio.
My most beautiful wife of 40 years, Mary, passed away from
cancer in 2018 and is with Jesus in heaven.
I have three children and two granddaughters.
The picture is of Mary and I at Northam Park during a brisk,
colorful autumn day in October of 2012.
I joined the Catholic Church in 1994 and needless to say I am
enjoying my relationship with Jesus Christ.

If you want to know the love and mercy that God has for you, then this book is for you!
And don't keep it to yourself! Share it with others – it's a great way to give your loved ones
a powerful sampling of the messages our Lord gave to St. Faustina and Sister Josefa.
I hope that many will find peace, consolation, and a deep desire to share this message with
others – because our world is more in need of God's love and mercy than ever.

Peggy (Blaha) Wolock
Catholic
St. Timothy Church, Columbus, Ohio, USA

A man who loves the Lord is obeying his call to renew two books written in the
20th century by faithful daughters of God. God's words and deeds of yesterday remain
true today. They are God's truths. Mark is a simple man with great faith and love for God.
I know because I am his friend in Christ.

Judith A. Anderson
Ecumenical
The Vineyard Church, Galena, Ohio, USA

I have finished working through the book and enjoyed it. I used it for personal prayer.
Overall, I think this is a good "taste" of the writings of these mystics and it leaves a
desire for more.

In Christ,
Fr. Tim Hayes
St Timothy Church, Columbus, Ohio, USA

ISBN 0615431109 $12.00
51200
9 780615 431109